PREACHING
FROM THE
INSIDE OUT

PREACHING
FROM THE
INSIDE
OUT

Charles B. Bugg

BROADMAN PRESS
NASHVILLE, TENNESSEE

4220-03

ISBN: 0-8054-2003-7

Dewey Decimal Classification: 251
Subject Heading: PREACHING
Library of Congress Catalog Card Number: 92-6337
Printed in the United States of America

Scripture quotations marked NIV are from the Holy Bible, *New International Version,* copyright © 1973, 1978, 1984 by International Bible Society. Used by permission. Scripture marked KJV is from the *King James Version.*

Library of Congress Cataloging-in-Publication Data
Bugg, Charles B.
  Preaching from the inside out / Charles B. Bugg.
    p. cm.
  ISBN 0-8054-2003-7
  1. Preaching. I. Title.
  BV4211.2.B867   1992
  251— dc20   92-6337
                                                                  CIP

FOREWORD

The reader of this volume will soon discover that the experience of the book is that of listening to Professor Bugg talk to his students about preaching. Even when he is talking *about* his students, the professor is talking *to* his students. In other words, this book is conversational.

What does it mean that a book is conversational in its style? Does it mean that the language is informal, even casual? Not necessarily, even though in this case the language is consciously made accessible to the reader who is approaching the pulpit, perhaps with more than enough awe and apprehension. Does it mean the pages are lacking in real substance, a passing the time with off-the-the-top-of-the-head opinions? It could, but not in this case. The perceptive reader will find here easy access to much reading, reflection, experience, and prayer.

In its best sense, conversational means three things: First, the partners in conversation have enough in common to be able to communicate. This volume certainly meets that criterion. Professor Bugg and his students share a love and respect for the ministry of preaching. Second, the partners have their own identities, backgrounds, and convictions so that the conversation can be real and potentially fruitful. It is not a game of echo. There is enough difference between a professor and a student that a genuine conversation can occur. Finally, conversation takes place if each is willing to learn from the other. We can safely assume that some of the students desire to learn and are open to ideas. As for this professor, he is also a student. Not all professors are students of their students, but Professor Bugg listens and a good idea from a student is no less a good idea.

A genuine conversation is an occasion of mutual vulnerability. Frankly, I was surprised at Professor Bugg's willingness to share so much of himself: his fears as well as his faith, his failures as well as his successes, his doubts as well as his certainties, his demons as well as his angels. But such is the mark of a teacher. The teacher, says Kierkegaard, is a servant, and the servant submits to being bent into the shape necessary for learning to take place.

Fred B. Craddock

CONTENTS

PART I

PREACHING FROM INSIDE OUR CONTEXT

1

SPEAKING FROM INSIDE OUR DEPTHS

I will never forget the night of my ordination to the ministry. The church was my "home church," where I had accepted Jesus Christ as my personal Savior, where I had been baptized, and where I had been nurtured in the faith. I was among people who had loved me and who had encouraged me in my spiritual journey.

At the end of the service, I stood at the front of the church as the people came by to say their parting words. I will never forget one elderly woman who had been such an encouragement to me. She assured me of her love and prayers, but her last words are the ones that I will never forget. "Just preach Jesus," she said, and that was her benediction to me.

What a benediction that was! After many years, I still carry powerful memories of her well-founded admonition. Preaching that makes a difference leaves people in the presence of Another. Our task as proclaimers is to bring people into the presence of the God who has fully revealed Himself in the person of Jesus Christ. Otherwise, our proclamation may be good advice or nice words, but it does not produce transformation of lives. "Just preach Jesus," that dear woman said to me. She had no degree in homiletics, but her advice was as profound as I have ever gotten or given in a seminary preaching class.

I thought about her words as I began to put this book together. The title, *Preaching from the Inside Out,* may suggest to some a lack of emphasis on the transcendent dimension in preaching. It may sound as if I am simply emphasizing the person of the preacher and am only calling for preachers to share more of themselves. There seems to be little "Jesus" here. On the surface it appears that I have not taken seriously those words of good advice, "Just preach Jesus."

If the title leaves that impression, I hope the contents will quickly change the reader's mind. One of the things I want to call for is a new emphasis on the spiritual vitality of the preacher. Preaching is more than a craft or an art or a profession. It is more than the shaping of some words designed to dazzle the ears of hearers. Preaching grows out of the minister's own experience with the living God. As preachers, we stand inside the faith. We are not objective. We bear witness to what has changed our lives.

A key word is *relationship*. Preaching cannot be separated from all that a minister is. The concept that we just "get up" a sermon fails to take seriously all of the factors that converge in the person who is preaching. Preaching cannot be separated from the person of the preacher.

Our Relationship with God

Out of all the relationships that we have as ministers, none is more vital than our relationship with God. Yet, many books on preaching include nothing about the spiritual formation of the minister. Much is written about how to construct a sermon but little about how to construct the person who delivers the sermon. We are taught how to deliver a message but little about how that message is divinely delivered to us. We are instructed in how to shape sounds, but not much is said about the inner silence of the preacher in the divine Presence that should give birth to the sounds.

When we speak out of our depths, we begin with the assumption that those depths are the places where the living God meets us. Tragically, too many of us in the ministry spend too little time in the silence with God so that the sounds of our speaking are shaped out of that creative, renewing silence.

13

Too often we ministers plead busyness as the reason for little time spent in prayer and in our own spiritual formation. We find ourselves reacting to the demands of our church, and our ministry becomes a stream of ceaseless activity. What happens is that our inner life and the depth of our preaching suffer. We may continue to talk about God but very little with God, and soon the words that we speak take on a hollow, shallow ring.

Saying no to a request for our help as ministers is difficult for most of us. After all, one of the reasons that we became ministers was to help people. However, we have to learn that our physical, emotional, and spiritual resources are not inexhaustible. Thus, we need to set some limits, and we need to establish the priority of our relationship to God so that when we speak and minister, we have something to give.

Several years ago, I heard a well-known teacher of preaching make the statement, "Good preaching is a response." We know that preaching is a response to a human need or to a word from God that captures the preacher in some biblical text. More than that, good preaching is a response to the gracious, loving God who is the source and strength of all of our ministry. We recognize our dependence upon God. Our whole life becomes a response to this God who shares life in Jesus Christ. Our preaching of the Good News is a response to the Good News which we have heard and are hearing through His Spirit.

However, the busyness of our vocation sometimes causes us to say that we have no time to listen to God. Our constant closeness to the things of God can keep us from spending time with Him. If we are pastors, we spend much of our time at the church building. Almost everyday we are dealing with some aspect of the church, and sometimes we see the church at its worst. We must not assume that time spent with the things of God constitutes time spent with God.

When the risen Christ wrote to the church at Ephesus in the Book of Revelation, He commended the Ephesian Christians on their good deeds, hard work, perseverance, and endurance. Amazingly, Jesus says to them that they have

not yet grown weary. Nevertheless, spiritual weariness does
not seem very far off, as Jesus admonished them in the next
paragraph. "Yet I hold this against you: You have forsaken
your first love. Remember the height from which you have
fallen! Repent and do the things which you did at first"
(Rev. 2:4-5, NIV).

Putting first things first is a challenge for those of us who
are ministers. While the words of the risen Christ in the
Book of Revelation are addressed to a church, they could
very well be spoken to a Monday morning pastor's confer-
ence. Which of us as a minister has not known the kind of
spiritual fatigue that comes from working for God without
taking time to let God work in us? Which of us has not also
known those times of trying to fashion sermons when there
have been no times of sacred silence in our lives?

In his lectures to students on preaching, Charles Spurgeon emphasized the centrality of prayer. Spurgeon said:

> The minister who does not earnestly pray over his work
> must surely be a vain and conceited man. He acts as if he
> thought himself sufficient of himself, and therefore
> needed not to appeal to God. Yet what a baseless pride to
> conceive that our preaching can ever be in itself so power-
> ful that it can turn men from their sins, and bring them to
> God without the working of the Holy Ghost.[1]

Another factor which has blurred the divine dimension of
preaching is the tendency to view proclamation strictly as a
craft. Attention is given only to the "horizontal" aspect of
preaching. How do we put together a sermon? What makes
for effective delivery? What are the needs of people, and
how do we address them? These are all vital questions, and
much is being written today on issues such as the forms
and delivery of a sermon. Research into how people listen
holds great promise for the preacher who wants to communicate more effectively. To speak of preaching as a craft is to
recognize the value of studying about preaching and the
fact that all of us can learn to preach better.

However, preaching is more than a craft. It is a calling from God; thus, the preacher places ultimate reliance upon the Spirit of God. While we may impress people with our own gifts, we realize that as ministers our goal is more than impression. We are not called to dazzle people with our rhetoric or to have them leave the sanctuary each Sunday impressed only with the style of the sermon.

Rather, the sermon is designed to bring people into the presence of God, and as such, it functions as an offering. The preacher must keep in mind through all the preparation, studying, and delivering of a sermon that if the message is going to change anybody's life, it will be because God blesses and uses it. Therefore, the minister views the sermon as an offering. The intent is to put our study, our preparation, and most of all, ourselves in God's hands.

Paul wrote about this act of surrendering ourselves in his first letter to the Corinthians. Pride was a major problem at Corinth. Admitting one's weaknesses or inadequacies was not done. Paul spoke about his own insufficiency, and in the process stressed the sufficiency of God in preaching:

> I came to you in weakness and fear, and with much trembling. My message and my preaching were not with wise and persuasive words, but with a demonstration of the Spirit's power, so that your faith might not rest on men's wisdom, but on God's power (1 Cor. 2:3-5, NIV).

This kind of honesty is liberating for those of us who preach. Paul was certainly not saying that he made no preparation and left it all to God. After we have done all that we can to get the sermon ready, we trust God to use it and to bless it. If people's lives are truly changed, it will not be because of the impressiveness of some preacher, but because the Spirit of God moves through the sermon to effect real change in the lives of the listeners.

Much of this book was written while I was on sabbatical leave at Candler Theological Seminary, which is a part of Emory University in Atlanta. When I arrived on the campus of this United Methodist seminary, I was assigned a desk in the rare book area of the theological library. While looking around one night, I saw in the corner an odd looking piece of furniture. I knew that it was old, but when I got closer and saw the inscription, I was in for a wonderful surprise: "Prayer Desk or Pulpit Made for John Wesley about 1740, Used by Him in Preaching to the Miners of Wales."

I found myself drawn to this sacred desk, and sometimes I stood behind it trying to envision the powerful sermons that were preached there. What also appealed to me was the part of the inscription that said, "Prayer Desk or Pulpit." Which was it? The desk had a place for Wesley to stand, but it also provided a railing where he could have knelt in prayer. Could this have been both a prayer desk and a pulpit? In Wesley's ministry, prayer and preaching were inextricably bound. Why not have a place where a preacher could both pray and proclaim?

Preaching from inside our depths demands those times of silence before God when we commit ourselves anew to Him and trust His presence and power in a new way. Only if the sounds of our sermons arise out of that sacred silence will there be word that will make lasting difference.

Our Relationship with Life Around Us

As ministers, our primary relationship is with God, but we also live and minister in the world where we are. Therefore, good preachers are not just good talkers; they are good observers of life. Opening our mouths before we open our eyes and ears leads to sermons that have little relationship to life.

Blessed is the congregation whose preacher has eyes that see and ears that hear. What is going on in the lives of the people to whom we preach? What are their joys, frustrations, hopes, dreams, fears, and nightmares? What makes them happy, sad, angry, or afraid? Where do they spend their time? What do they read, look at on television, or listen to on the radio?

When our children were very young, my wife and I vowed

that we would be "with it" parents. We had seen friends who were parents of teenagers being dismissed by their children as totally "out of it." Diane and I were determined to keep up with the music, styles, and fads of our children when they became teenagers. You probably have guessed what happened. Our best intentions failed, and it really was a relief that first time that my daughter looked at me and said, "Dad, you are really out of it."

Obviously, we cannot be everywhere, read everything, and understand everybody; but there is little excuse for the minister who seems to have no sense of the questions people are asking. One of the amazing things about the preaching of Jesus was the way that He connected God to the lives of His listeners. Jesus spoke about things that mattered, and He preached and taught in ways that even the simplest folks could understand. We do not know exactly how Jesus spent the years between the age of 12 and 30, but surely He listened to the deep needs of the people as He worked in Joseph's carpenter shop in Nazareth.

One of the most obvious aspects of our times is the spiritual hunger of many people. Go to any secular bookstore and notice the number of books that profess to offer enlightenment or encouragement for the journey of life. Despite unprecedented material prosperity in our nation, many people are desperately hungry to find something to fill the emptiness of their lives. People who are making a good living now want to find a life worth living. They have everything in their hands; they have nothing in their hearts; and they are searching for something with size and substance.

What does this say to our preaching? It means that we need to deal with things that make a difference. We need to speak about a gospel that provides purpose and power for life. There needs to be a certainty in our sound. As preachers we are called to speak about a Christ who does not make a little difference or some difference, but who makes all the difference. Our deepest hungers will not be fed by meringue and whip cream. People are hungry for something with substance. They want to follow someone like Jesus who said with certainty and assurance, "Follow me."

Our Relationship to the Scriptures

One of the most exciting developments in recent years has been a renewed emphasis on biblical preaching. It is encouraging to see the Bible used as the source and authority for sermons. As Fred Craddock observed: "Sermons not informed and inspired by Scripture are objects dislodged, orphans in the world, without mother or father."[2] In Chapter Five, I want to spend more time discussing how we as preachers move inside a text, but I wanted to mention it here because it is an important part of learning to preach from the depths.

To preach biblical sermons demands hard work, discipline, and time. It sometimes means struggling with a text until the blessing of insight comes, rather than racing off to the library to see how someone else has preached the sermon. The free church tradition has emphasized the doctrine of the "priesthood of all believers." In these churches preachers proclaim that each believer has access to the Scriptures and that each may interpret them as the Holy Spirit leads.

I want to recover the priesthood of the "priests." Many of us have come through school and have become intimidated by the experts. We do not trust our own encounter with the Bible; thus, our churches often miss the freshness that comes with the minister's own sense of wonder and discovery when led by the Holy Spirit.

We all get ideas from other people, but it is harmful when the preacher's first approach to a biblical text comes through someone else's interpretation. I will sometimes have students ask, "Is it wrong to preach someone else's sermon?" After all, we have all heard someone say, "When better sermons are written, I will preach them." My answer is, "Yes, it is absolutely wrong to preach someone else's sermon as yours." Not only is it plagiarism, but it also tends to establish a pattern where the minister misses any deep encounter with the Word of God. It is hard to speak from the depths when all we have is the sidelong glance at the opinions of others.

Our Relationship to Ourselves

Preaching from our depths presupposes that we believe that God has something to offer through us. It has much to do with the doctrine of grace. God has given each of us the gift of ourselves, and the best gift that I have to give is to offer who I am to God and to others.

In preaching, well-known ministers often become models. When I was growing up in the church, I looked to Billy Graham. I imitated his gestures and voice inflection. I even held my Bible the way that Billy Graham did and punctuated my sermons with the phrase, "The Bible says." Several people in my home church even said to me, "You are going to be the next Billy Graham."

Then I started meeting other young preachers who also sounded and looked like Billy Graham in the pulpit. I was confused. Which of us was going to be the next great evangelist? What was the problem? There is only one Billy Graham, and God has used his talents and commitment in an extraordinary way. As far as I know, none of us who were trying to be like him are still being talked about as the next Billy Graham.

A theological issue at stake involves having the grace to accept who I am as a gift from God. The minister who totally changes style, voice, and personality when walking into the pulpit is unintentionally saying, "I'm not good enough to be used by God. I have to be someone else."

We all are affected by preachers who have modeled effective delivery. By nature I am an intense preacher. I have learned much about storytelling and the pace of a sermon from preachers like Fred Craddock. African-American preachers have reminded me of the need of joy and celebration when I have taken myself too seriously. Learning from others, however, does not mean becoming their imitators.

Each of us has something to say. We have experienced

God in a multitude of different fashions. Christ has led in
His unique way. Each of us must lead in our unique ways.
When we preach from the inside out, we affirm that by
God's grace we have something to say, and no one else can
say it in just the same way. If our voice is not heard, the
world will be diminished. Persons are listening... for God
through us. I do not know anything more exciting than
that.

Exercises

I. In this chapter, I emphasized that our primary relation-
    ship as preachers is with God. I mentioned several
    things that keep us from developing this dimension of
    our lives. Think about your own life. What keeps you
    from spending time with God? List those things that
    take your time, and think about why they are impor-
    tant. Ask God to help you give yourself to what is most
    important.

II. Think about the needs that people have shared with you
    recently. Make a list of 3 or 4 of these needs, and then
    select a biblical passage that addresses each concern. In
    one sentence, what does the Bible say to that need?

Notes

1. Charles H. Spurgeon, *Spurgeon's Lectures to His Students*. ed.
David Otis Fuller (Grand Rapids: Zondervan Publishing House, 1945),
44.

2. Fred B. Craddock, *Preaching* (Nashville: Abingdon Press, 1985), 27.

2

THE INSIDE WAY
OF PREACHING

Homiletics, or the study of preaching, is hardly an exact science. Humanly speaking, preaching is more akin to art than science. Therefore, much of the beauty is in the eye of the beholder.

Go to any town or city and ask, "Who is the best preacher in this place?" You will get a variety of responses. Some people like the conversational delivery of their minister. Others seem to need a preacher who shouts and perspires. Some like narrative sermons, while others just want the facts. Unless a sermon has clearly spelled out "points," it is not really preaching to these folks. The beauty of a sermon is largely in the eyes of the beholder. Teachers of preaching are presumptuous to tell their students that there is only one way to preach.

Those of us who preach and who try to teach preaching have some specific concepts we believe are important in communicating the reality of God in Jesus Christ: inadequacy, incarnation, intensity, intimacy, and integrity. Whatever style or form a sermon may take, these things are central in proclamation. They are a vital part of preaching from the inside out.

Inadequacy

Preaching begins with the confession of the minister: "What I am trying to do in this sermon is impossible to me. Only through the power of God can the life of anyone be

22

changed." In his Lyman Beecher Lectures on preaching, Gardner Taylor spoke eloquently about what he called, "The Presumptuousness of Preaching":

> Measured by almost any gauge, preaching is a presumptuous business. If the undertaking does not have some sanctions beyond human reckoning, then it is, indeed, rash and audacious for one person to dare to stand up before or among other people and declare that he or she brings from the Eternal God a message for those who listen which involves issues nothing less than those of life and death.[1]

Those of us who preach can understand the reluctance of Moses when God told him to be the spokesperson for the nation of Israel. How could he stand before the authorities of Egypt and tell Pharaoh to let God's people go? "Moses said to the Lord, 'O Lord, I have never been eloquent, neither in the past nor since you have spoken to your servant. I am slow of speech and tongue'" (Ex. 4:10, NIV).

A part of our sense of inadequacy comes from our awareness as ministers that we need the very message that we preach. When Jesus began His own ministry, according to Luke, He stood up in the synagogue and read from the prophet Isaiah:

> The Spirit of the Lord is on me, because he has anointed me to preach good news to the poor. He has sent me to proclaim freedom for the prisoners and recovery of sight for the blind, to release the oppressed, to proclaim the year of the Lord's favor (Luke 4:18-19, NIV).

Those words became the road map for Jesus' ministry and the focus of His preaching in Luke. Throughout the Gospel of Luke, Jesus reached to those who were impoverished, imprisoned, blinded, and oppressed by the sin, structures, and situations of the world around them.

These words of Jesus can be read by ministers today as the keynote of their preaching. Times have changed, but we still speak to people who are struggling with the sin, structures, and suffering of life. People make their way to our churches wanting to know if we have a word of faith or freedom, a word of hope or help for the often difficult journey of life. Preachers are also a part of the struggle and sin themselves. We do not stand above the battle. As preachers we receive no inoculations at our ordinations that keep us from the same difficulties that others face. Thus, we are both hearer and speaker of every sermon we preach. The word is not just from us; it is also for us.

To affirm the Bible as the Word of God does not mean that we have appropriated every word as reality for our lives. Quite frankly, there are parts of the Bible before which I stand, and my response is, "Lord, I believe! Help Thou my unbelief!"

For example, I have preached many sermons on those powerful words of Paul to the Romans: "And we know that in all things God works for the good of those who love him, who have been called according to his purpose" (Rom. 8:28, NIV). Those are words that I have learned to love. The great apostle seems to have the faith that God is able to take even the broken pieces of our lives and shape them into God's providential plan for each of us.

As a pastor, I would often preach from this text because I knew that many folks were struggling to make sense of the sufferings and setbacks of their lives. Most of us grew up with a dream for our lives. What happens when the dream dies and the picture that we had envisioned for ourselves falls at our feet in a thousand jagged pieces? I like the assurance of Paul, "and we know that in all things God works."

Then one February afternoon in a hospital room in Augusta, Georgia, my wife and I received the news from the physician that our ten year old son was critically ill. Suddenly, our family was thrust into a world of operating rooms, radiation treatments, and suffering that made the whole world seem as if it were covered with a dark cloud.

"And we know..." Paul wrote, but suddenly I found myself

not knowing. Our family had tried to love God the best we knew how, and we thought we had been called according to His purpose. However, when I watched my son endure such suffering, it was hard even to keep preaching.

The year of the diagnosis was 1983. The perspective of time and the partial recovery of our son has helped to restore my sense of hope. However, I now preach from Romans 8:28 in a new way. I am there to speak the words, but I am also there to hear the word from God again that life does have purpose. For me to speak about suffering is to speak about something that has touched the depths of my life. When I preach, I also pray that I will be touched by God in the depths of my pain for my prayer is, "Lord, I believe! Help thou my unbelief!"

Which of us called to preach is really worthy to speak the word of God to the lives of people? Is anybody alone sufficient for such a thing? What alarms me the most in a preaching class is to encounter students who have just enough gifts to feel that they can go it alone. Just give them an audience, and the words flow easily, too easily.

Preachers have a calling from God that is both wonderful and overwhelming. Nobody has any greater privilege than to stand before people week after week and speak about God's love in Christ and the things that matter most. None of us is adequate for what we are called to be. Every moment of every day needs to be lived with a deep sense of our dependence upon the power and provision of God.

Incarnation

Preachers deal with words. Words are the tools of our trade. We take words seriously. Words can make a difference. "I love you." Just three words—two pronouns with an intervening verb. When put together and spoken to us, some of our lives have been changed forever.

Consider the words, "I don't love you." Just words? Hardly! Do you feel the pain, the rejection, the hurt? Some lives are never the same again because somebody said, "I don't love you."

Words do have enormous power, and preachers believe that words can change people's lives forever. Our human words become the vehicle through which God communicates the divine Word, God's Son, to the world.

The coming of God into the world in human flesh is called the incarnation. In Jesus Christ, God entered this world in a way that God never has before and never will again. Because of this supreme revelation of God, we dare to preach that God cannot be fully known apart from accepting Jesus of Nazareth as personal Savior and Lord.

During His earthly ministry Jesus modeled for us incarnational preaching and teaching. The God about whom He spoke was a God that He knew intimately as "Abba" (Father). The truth that Jesus preached was not just something that He had been told, but it was something that He had experienced. In fact, Matthew recorded that when Jesus had finished the Sermon on the Mount, the crowd responded more to the *way* he taught than to *what* he taught: "When Jesus had finished saying these things, the crowds were amazed at his teaching, because he taught as one who had authority, and not as their teachers of the law" (Matt. 7:28-29, NIV). Apparently, what impressed the crowd was the "freshness" of Jesus' message. Other rabbis quoted one authority after another to support their positions, but Jesus taught as if this was "His" message. And, of course, it was.

How do we then speak with that kind of freshness and authority? The message must be ours. That does not suggest that we have appropriated all of the good news of the Bible for ourselves or that we have experienced all of God for ourselves. People have a difficult time relating to a preacher who seems to have "arrived" in the spiritual life and has no room to grow.

People want to hear from a preacher who is seeking to internalize the message, and who speaks out of the depths of life. We want to hear a message that seems real to the person who is speaking it. No matter how eloquent the preacher is, the words are "sounding brass and a tinkling cymbal" (1 Cor. 13:1, KJV) if we do not sense that the preacher is genuine and authentic.

Those who teach preaching need to be careful to help students craft more than sermons. We need to help craft persons themselves. The fact is that much of our communication takes place at a level other than words. When I listen to someone, I am listening to more than what that person says. I am listening to *the* person. Likewise, when I listen to someone preach, I am certainly listening to more than a sermon. Is this person genuine? Does this preacher have an authority that comes from a relationship with Christ? Do the words seem to spring from the lips or out of a life's encounter with the living God? How I answer these questions will determine how I listen.

According to Matthew, when the people heard Jesus, they did not comment about the substance of the sermon or even the moving words of the message. Instead, the people praised Jesus' authority. His message arose out of His relationship to God. Jesus' words had power because He had power.

None of us can incarnate the message as Jesus did, but we can learn from His model of ministry. Central to Jesus' life was the balance between speaking *for* God and speaking *to* God. While the ministry of Jesus was relatively short, He never seemed to be in a rush. He had time for people; He spoke to people; and we remember the words. For example, who could forget a story that made grace so alive: "There was a man who had two sons" (Luke 15:11, NIV). We remember the demand of discipleship on the day that Jesus said to a would-be follower: "Follow me, and let the dead bury their own dead" (Matt. 8:23, NIV).

We remember Jesus in those times when He spoke for God, addressing the difficulties and decisions in the lives of people. When we read the Gospels, we remember Him also for those times when He listened to God. Jesus seemed to need those times when His own spirit was fashioned and formed, when He was "alone with the Alone."

As ministers we often overlook our own *being* in the

pressure of our *doing*. The result is a loss of freshness and vitality in our preaching. We may keep saying words, but the words sound distant because God seems distant. To preach incarnationally means that we must create those times when we can be alone with God and have our own being renewed. After all, people are listening more to who we are than to what we say.

Intensity

What is intensity in preaching? Perhaps, I should begin by saying what I do not mean by this word. I do not mean that the preacher is always serious either in the preparation or in the delivery of the sermon. A sense of humor is a powerful tool for any minister. Certainly the minister is not called to be a stand-up comedian, but a preacher who is always solemn and serious in the delivery of a sermon usually is too intense for a congregation. Most of us like some "contrast" in the sermons that we hear. We listen better if there are changes in the pace and type of material in a sermon. We need times when we plunge the depths of life, but we also need moments when we can laugh at life.

Jonah, sitting under the shade of the vine feeling sorry for himself, is both serious and funny. The prophet had preached, and the entire population of Nineveh had been converted. What if you or I had preached that revival? I would be hard to live with for awhile. I would say to my friends, "Do you know what happened in my last revival? Why, the entire city from the mayor to the maid was converted." This would be a real test for any preacher's humility.

What did Jonah do? Revel in the success? Rejoice that so many have come to know God? No, Jonah sulked and told God that he did not even like the people of Nineveh and that he really was angry that they had turned to God. This is both serious and funny. Jonah represents the spirit of exclusion, the attitude that God is only for "me and mine." If the spirit of Jonah were to prevail, missions and evangelism would be eliminated except for "our kind." Obviously, the Book of Jonah deals with an issue that drives to the heart of our faith: Is the salvation of God for everybody?

While the Book of Jonah is concerned with serious business, it also conveys the message in a way that makes us laugh at the pouting prophet as well as ourselves. The contrast between what is and what should be is startling. Jonah preached, and the whole city was saved. Any preacher would be overjoyed, but not Jonah. People came to God. Is that not what every follower of God should want? Not Jonah! The Ninevites were the wrong people. Jonah despised them for the pain that they had inflicted on his people, and the last thing that he wanted for his enemies was the blessing of God. Jonah never did get the message from God. The last words of the prophet were, " 'I am angry enough to die'" (Jonah 4:9, NIV).

A preacher needs to enter a biblical text and see not only the words but also feel the texture and emotions of a passage. The Bible is a book that makes us cry and makes us laugh. Its pages become a mirror in which we see ourselves reflected; sometimes that recognition brings a frown, and sometimes it brings a smile. Intensity does not mean that when I preach I assume a somber mood. The pulpit is not a place where only a sober and solemn face is appropriate.

Intensity is a passion for the message that we preach. This passion comes from the awareness that God uses the foolishness of preaching to speak to the lives of people and that what we preach can change the lives of our listeners.

Preaching makes a difference! In fact, it makes all the difference in the lives of people, and we need to approach our calling with the sense that what we do as preachers is the most important thing in all the world.

I have heard ministers say, "Oh, I'm just a preacher." What does that convey? "I'm harmless. Other people have jobs that make a difference, but I just talk, and nobody seems to listen anyway." Some of this attitude may grow out of the pejorative way that the word *preaching* is sometimes used. "Don't preach to me," somebody says, and the impression is that preaching is scolding and talking down to people.

The idea that preaching makes little difference in the lives of people also comes from the way we ministers have sometimes approached preaching. If we stand up on Sunday and are unprepared, we give the impression that preaching is unimportant. If we approach the task of preaching as if we are just speaking words that few people hear and that make no difference, our proclamation will lack power.

Several years ago I preached a revival at a church in Florida. At the end of the last service, an elderly woman came by and said, "This revival has changed my life." Do you know what my inner reaction was? "You're kidding. Those were just words that I was speaking. How could they change your life?"

Fortunately, I did not say those things to her. But I thought to myself afterwards: *I teach preaching at a seminary; I tell students that they have no greater calling than to preach the gospel; I tell them that God can take our words and use them to change the lives of people. All of these things I say in a passionate way, but when an elderly woman said, "This revival has changed my life," I started to respond, "But I was just preaching."*

Perhaps, every minister should have inscribed on the pulpit, "What I am doing makes all the difference." It may keep us from the deadly attitude that we are not really heard or if we are heard, we are not taken seriously. Who knows whether the words we speak may be the vehicle through which God makes the difference in somebody's life. George Buttrick spoke powerfully at the end of his first Lyman Beecher Lecture on preaching. Talking about "The Preacher's Place Today," Buttrick concluded:

> Christian preaching, poor words glimmering with soul, can give men the glimpse of another world. Men will come (if the preacher is faithful) from those pleasures without which they might also be happy, from their business which chokes them with dust, from their gnawing memory of sin, from the senseless clamor and grasping of the day; they will come hungering for the glimpse of God.

Even one glimpse will save them: they will know there is another Country, with its mountains of rectitude, its rivers of cleansing grace, its deep sky of the ideal life, its little flowers of an agelong mercy. Of all the tasks of earth this Love is best—the Love of God in the face of Christ. Jesus came preaching. Let the preacher count it all joy that he, too, may preach.[2]

Intimacy

Have you ever listened to a preacher and thought, "That person is talking to me"? The room may have been crowded with other people, but you felt that the message had your name on it. Something about the preacher, the words, the style, the substance of the sermon—something made you feel that the message was for you. That is *intimacy* in preaching.

There is no magical formula to make intimacy a part of every sermon. Some ministers have a gift for conveying warmth and personal concern in their preaching. It is a reflection of their personalities and the ability to convey something of themselves to people. While there is no seminary course designed to teach a minister how to move from distance to intimacy, we can do some things that will help to communicate ourselves and our message.

How we prepare a sermon is vital. If we are taught that the preparation of a sermon is carefully crafting a series of words, then we spend most of our time putting the sermon together. We prepare a manuscript or a lengthy outline, leaving little time to get the sermon off the pages and into our own lives. We do not internalize the message, and our preaching becomes the delivering of a string of words, rather than a message that has encountered us.

Please do not hear this as an excuse for poor preparation. Neither is this a rationale for preachers not giving careful thought to the way something is said. Rather, it is an appeal to see the sermon as a whole. When we go into the pulpit, we should not be preoccupied with which word follows which. Avoid the attitude of anxiously waiting to speak that powerful phrase so carefully crafted in the study. Our primary purpose is not to impress the congregation with the way that we can use words, but it is to convey a message. The preacher should ask, "What am I trying to say in this sermon? What is the message? What do I need to hear from God in this biblical text, and what do I want the congregation to hear that may change all our lives?"

We all have different ways of preparing the message. I have known some preachers who work very effectively with manuscripts. I encourage young preachers to write out their sermons for awhile in order to refine their styles and sharpen their use of language. Written sermons encourage more precision in targeting the message and avoiding the danger of the sermon that wanders all over the world but goes nowhere in particular.

My own belief is that after a preacher has developed a style and become more at home in the pulpit, it is better not to use a manuscript or extensive notes. The primary transaction in preaching is often between the preacher and the notes rather than between the preacher and the congregation. If we use a manuscript, we are usually tempted to look down at the end of a paragraph and the beginning of a new one. These places are often where we have included some of our most pivotal material. Precisely at the point that we need to communicate with all of ourselves, our eyes have lost contact with the congregation because we wanted to say everything in the sequence in which it was written.

Another factor in the preparation stage of a manuscript that hinders intimacy is that most of us are trained to write for the eye and not for the ear. We have learned to write term papers filled with technical words and ample documentation. If somebody does not understand what we have written, then he or she may reread and hopefully get it on the second or third try.

Most of our sermons have one chance to reach the ear. Lengthy sentences, complicated words, extensive quoting of so-called authorities—all of these make listening more difficult. Most of the writing that we are trained to do in school stresses reason and logic. Certainly, a sermon should not be unreasonable and illogical. A sermon needs logic to its content and form in order that people can follow and understand its message.

While we want to be logical, most of the time we want to avoid argumentation in a sermon. Much of the writing we have been trained to do has been to try to present a point of view aimed at convincing the mind of the reader. We usually do not employ images, illustrations, or stories to appeal to the heart of our reader. After all, a term paper is designed to appeal to the cognitive side of the reader.

A sermon, however, is designed to change people's lives, and that involves an appeal to both mind and heart. The use of images and stories is often the most effective way to help people hear and see what God can do in their lives. Jesus certainly illustrated that in Luke 15. What is the grace of God like? Jesus responded with three unforgettable stories. The grace of God is like a shepherd who goes to retrieve a lost sheep, a woman who turns her house upside down to find a lost coin, and a father who more than anything else wants his two sons to know the joy of "coming home." Jesus did not present an argument for grace. He painted three pictures, and what is seen and heard is the story of "Amazing Grace."

Whether we write a manuscript or not, we need to keep in mind that there is a difference in writing a paper that will be read with the eyes and a sermon that will be heard with the ears. When we use long sentences, complicated words, and speak only to the minds of our listeners, we may be perceived as distant and aloof. People may compliment their pastor for being intelligent, but they will not "feel" what their preacher is saying. In my opinion, good preachers speak to both the head and the heart because almost every important decision or change that we make in life is made with all of our being.

In the delivery stage of the sermon, several factors are important in creating intimacy. We must keep in mind that the most important transaction is between the preacher and the hearers, not between the preacher and the notes.

Eye contact is important. A face that is consistent with the message of the minister is vital. Most of us have heard sermons on joy delivered by preachers with scowls on their faces. On the other hand, the preacher who talks about the death of a child with a plastic smile will confuse the congregation. I ask the students in my preaching classes to ponder the question, "What do I want my listeners to *feel* in this sermon?"

Most of us are trained to ask, "What ideas do I want them to hear?" That often leads to the kind of preaching that is only concerned with communicating concepts in a detached sort of way. I need to think through my sermon, but I also need to feel through it before I deliver it. Somebody told me that the inscription on the pulpit at the First Baptist Church, Newport, Kentucky, reads, "What do you want to do to these people?" I do not know the history of the choice of those words, but it reflects a strong understanding of preaching. Words not only say things but also *do* things in the lives of people. As preachers we need to think through our sermon and also feel through it. What am I trying to say, and what am I trying to do through this message?

Tone of voice is important in the capacity to create intimacy. Again, we need to think and feel through the sermon before we deliver it. For example, I am going to preach the story of Jesus in the Garden of Gethsemane. Here was the last night of Jesus' earthly life, and He prayed. It is a story of anguish and agony, struggle and surrender, and of disciples who keep falling asleep because of their own grief at what was happening to them and to their Leader.

Should this story be shouted? Hardly. You and I as pastors do not walk into the hospital room where a parishioner is dying and start shouting and screaming. We are sensitive to the mood of the situation; similarly the mood of the text will help determine how we deliver the sermon.

Preachers need to operate within the range of their own voice. I have a bass voice. Ministers with a higher pitch voice can do some things in their preaching that would sound foolish and contrived if I tried them. We try to maintain consistency in the way we use our voice in public and in private so that the people who hear us will not think we have been transformed into someone else in the pulpit. Nothing is more inauthentic than preachers who think they have to *sound* like a preacher when they get into the pulpit. Why not sound like ourselves because we are the ones that God has called to preach?

This does not prohibit us from being dynamic in the pulpit. In fact, one question that pastor search committees frequently ask me about potential ministers is, "Are they dynamic?" Our dynamic should spring out of our own selves, out of our encounter with the biblical text, and out of our deep conviction that more than anything else, the word of God needs to be heard. If we try to manufacture a dynamic delivery, we usually wind up looking and sounding overly dramatic and affected. If I walk into the pulpit believing that what I have to say is vitally important to me and to the congregation, I will find that a dynamic delivery within the framework of my personality and gifts will come from the inside out.

Integrity

It is important to remind ourselves as preachers that much communication happens at a level other than through the words we speak. People are listening to us, and they are making judgments about our credibility, sincerity, and authenticity. In a pastoral relationship, the awareness by people of who we are is heightened by the fact that we live, move, and have our being among them. Therefore, when we stand to speak, we are preaching against the backdrop of the lives that we live. People listen to us throughout the week as well as to our sermons on Sunday.

Integrity is the word to describe the consistency between the message that the minister speaks and the life that person lives. Our character as ministers is important. Our morals and ethics are vital. People look at the minister to represent in life the things about which that minister speaks.

Furthermore, if preaching does take place from the inside out, then we as ministers need to have experience with God in Christ whom we preach as central to life. Nothing would be more fatiguing or frustrating to a minister than to be called to give strong voice to matters that no longer make much difference. That is why the crafting of ourselves as preachers and persons under God is more important than the crafting of a sermon. That is why spiritual formation has become such a vital part of the curriculum in training ministers. We may send preachers from the seminary with all of the professional skills, but what if they leave with no hunger to know God more deeply? What if we teach them how to relate to people, but do little to help them in their continuing relationship to God? The stories are legend of outstanding ministers with superb gifts who one day decided that they had nothing more to say and walked out of the pulpit.

Some may interpret the word *integrity* to mean perfection. After all, some people expect their ministers to be perfect. Of course, no one of us is perfect, only imperfect in different ways. Therefore, we do not preach as if we have arrived spiritually and have appropriated all of the truth for ourselves.

Integrity may mean that you and I come to a biblical text admitting that we do not understand or have not experienced all that the passage means. In fact, it is presumptuous for any preacher to preach all of the Bible as if having total understanding of everything. The Bible is a book of comfort and discomfort. While we affirm all of it as the Word of God for us, we certainly do not pretend that we have incorporated it all into our lives.

Sermons on marriage and the family have a way of quickly bringing me face to face with my limits. My family knows me better than anyone else. It is embarrassing as I stand up to preach my month-long series on home and the family. I read Ephesians 5:25 (NIV), "Husbands, love your wives, just as Christ loved the church and gave himself up for her," and I look at my wife on the fifth row. Diane knows that I love her, but even in my finest moments at home, I am never compared to Christ.

Then I come to Ephesians 6:4 (NIV), "Fathers, do not

exasperate your children; instead, bring them up in the training and instruction of the Lord." I look at the faces of my two children. They have brought me enormous joy; no father could be prouder of the way that his children have turned out. But they know and I know about those times when I did not listen to them or responded to them with inappropriate anger, and they were exasperated.

For me to stand to preach on the family as if I am the perfect husband and parent is hypocritical. Maybe that is the reason that most of us males prefer to preach about Paul's instructions to the wives and children. That way our hypocrisy is not so apparent.

Whenever I preach from a text such as Genesis 22, I also have to confess some of my struggle to understand the ways of God. According to the account, God tested Abraham by asking him to take Isaac to the mountain and to offer him as a sacrifice. I know that the story turns out well and that both father and son came down the mountain together. I realize that this is a powerful passage about the radical obedience of Abraham, and the question for us is, "Are we that radically obedient to the call and claims of God?"

Yet I am bothered by those words, "God tested Abraham" and have to confess that I certainly do not understand all that means. Why would God ask people to give up their children to test their faith? Does this mean that God causes bad things to happen to good people to see if those people are really as good as they seem? This story raises some serious questions about the relationship of God to suffering, and to preach it from the inside out is to admit that I do not understand it all.

I am convinced that most people are turned off by preachers who seem to have pat answers to all of life's questions. I am also convinced that for preachers to pretend that we understand all mysteries, have all knowledge, and never "look through the glass darkly," is to try to become something that God never intended us to be.

Most people are not looking for perfection in their ministers. In fact, most of us have trouble identifying with people who seem to know it all and who would make us think that they receive "A+" in every area of life. At the same time, we do want a minister who takes God seriously both in Word and in life. That is integrity. We want to know that the Christ whom the preacher claims can make all the difference is making a difference to the life of the preacher. Then when the minister speaks, we know that we are listening to someone who is speaking to us from the inside out.

Exercises

I. Each of us operates with some assumptions based on our view of preaching. We may call this our "theology of preaching." Think for a few minutes, and then write down some words or ideas that shape the way you approach preaching.

II. Think about a preacher whom you admire. Make a list of the attributes you find worthy in that person. Describe the preacher's tone of voice, face, gestures, and other characteristics you recall.

III. Is there a particular passage of Scripture that stretches your faith and challenges you in some area of your life? Try to move inside that text and ask, "If I really believed this, what difference would it make in the way I live?"

Notes

1. Gardner C. Taylor, *How Shall They Preach* (Elgin, Ill.: Progressive Baptist Publishing House, 1977), 24.

2. George Buttrick, *Jesus Came Preaching: Christian Preaching in the New Age* (Grand Rapids: Baker Book House, 1931), 25-26.

3

PREACHING
INSIDE OUR TIMES

When I was a student in third grade, I had a teacher who called the names on the class roll every day. Her instructions were clear. We were all to answer, "Here." One student in the class delighted in being different. Whenever his name was called he responded, "Present." The teacher scowled, the rest of us snickered, but this student insisted on being present instead of here.

I want to thank my classmate, not for his behavior but for giving me an important word, "Present." Presence is important in preaching. Presence to the biblical text; presence to the congregation; presence to the Spirit of God—all of these are integral to effective proclamation.

In this chapter, I want to speak about another kind of presence—the presence of those who preach to the world in which they live. How that world is shaped affects two central things in preaching: content and delivery.

The presence of the preacher to the world helps to shape the content of the sermon. The preacher stands as bridge-builder between the Word of God and the world of the people to whom the minister speaks. Preachers study the Bible to try to find the Word of God; but unless they relate it to the lives of people, it is usually not heard. When we listen to a sermon, most of us want something that will feed our spirits. The world is filled with its disappointments and its discouragements. When we sit in the pew, we want a word for the living of our days and nights. Preaching that is not biblical is impotent. It lacks power. Preaching that is not connected to the lives of its listeners is irrelevant. It lacks purpose. Therefore, preachers need to know both the *sense* and *significance* of the text. We need to know the *what* and the *so what*. What is the truth that we want to speak, and why is it important?

Knowing the times in which we preach affects not only the *what* of the sermon but also the *how* of the sermon. How do people listen? We are now raising a generation of people in our churches whose primary way of receiving information is the television. They have grown up on images. They have seen things as well as heard things. We need to try to say things in such a way that we give people mental images. As I prepare a sermon, I must ask myself, "How can I image this in such a way that folks will hear and see it?"

Knowing both the Word and the world is imperative for a minister. A word of caution needs to be added. The world is constantly changing, and a good preacher stays alert to those changes. Nothing is sadder than a minister who is answering questions that nobody else is still asking. Few things are more detrimental to communication than to become stuck in a style of delivery that once was well-received but now seems outmoded and old-fashioned.

I want us to look at four needs that I believe are a part of our world today and which need to be taken seriously by those who preach.

Need for Certainty

If any word describes our times, it is the word, *uncertainty.* We live in a world of incredible change. Information multiplies at a staggering rate. We can identify with the cartoon of the two college students who were coming out of the campus library. One of them turned to the other and said, "Everyday, there are more and more things to be ignorant about."

Rapid advances in science and technology have brought us great benefits. None of us, for example, would want to go back to the way that medicine was practiced a hundred

years ago or even ten years ago. We are all grateful for the
strides that have been made in so many areas. But science
and technology, as wonderful as their benefits are, do not
tell us the meaning of life. That is the question for which we
Christians claim to have the ultimate answer.

Recently, I was in an airport. Some members of a religious cult were calling out to all who passed to stop and
listen to what they had to say. I watched as several people
paused to talk with the attractive young woman and man
who were tending the booth. What is it that draws people to
listen to this type of thing? Why is it that the shelves of
most secular book stores are filled with books that promise
fulfillment to lives that are empty? We are all searching for
some certainty in our lives. In a world of flux, is there
someone beyond ourselves in whom we can place our faith?
Where is the certainty in an uncertain world?

Our family had gone to the beach one day when our
children were younger. I will never forget standing at the
edge of the ocean and looking out at the horizon where the
sea and sky seem to meet. My children were standing on
either side of me looking at the same horizon. Suddenly, one
of them raised a life-size question: "Dad, is that all there is
to the world?" Since that was all that could be seen with the
eye, the conclusion was, "That's all there is."

Preachers dare to stand up each Sunday and speak to
people who are surrounded by complexity, change, and confusion. Many people wonder, "Is this all there is to life?"
Our message is that there is more, far more. We may not see
God with our eyes, but by faith we believe that God is alive
and at work in our world.

People need to hear a certain sound from the pulpit. They
need to know that not everything is relative. There are
some truths in life that stay the same. Most of all, people
need to know about the God in Christ who is the same
yesterday, today, and all the days of our lives.

Paul is a good example of this kind of certainty. Certain
things that the apostle knew sustained him in the stormy
stretches of his life. To the church at Rome, Paul wrote,

"And we know that in all things God works for the good of those who love him, who have been called according to his purpose" (Rom. 8:28, NIV). One of the apostle Paul's deepest convictions was that God was able to take the most jagged pieces of our lives and fit them into His providential picture. Paul was not saying that everything that happens to us is good. His fervent belief was that, if we loved God and were trying to live according to God's purpose, God would use everything for our good. Paul said it is something that "we know."

The pastoral epistle of 2 Timothy has another example of sustaining knowledge. "That is why I am suffering as I am. Yet I am not ashamed, because I know whom I have believed, and am convinced that he is able to guard what I have entrusted to him for that day" (2 Tim. 1:12, NIV). Being a Christian does not mean receiving inoculation against the sufferings of life. Preaching that promises to its followers a bigger house, better income, and the best of everything is false, creating tragic disillusionment. The certainty is that Christ is with us. Who we know is what counts; no matter what happens, we know that we can trust Him.

A word of caution is needed about this matter of certainty, and again Paul is our teacher. In that beautiful love chapter of 1 Corinthians 13, the apostle wrote, "Now we see but a poor reflection as in a mirror; then we shall see face to face. Now I know in part; then I shall know fully, even as I am fully known" (v. 12, NIV). The Corinthian church had some people who were too sure about everything. They thought they had the answers to all the questions, but in the process, they had lost the spirit of love. Paul confessed that he did not understand all of the mysteries of his faith and that he could not wrap his words around all the ways of God. The preacher needs to balance humility with the certainty that there is a God, He has given Himself to us in Jesus Christ, and He is alive and at work in the world through His Spirit.

Every minister ought to spend some time on the pediatric

oncology unit of a hospital. We have much to learn from children with cancer and their families. They teach us about courage and hope and even joy in the face of a devastating diagnosis. They also teach those who preach about the danger of offering pat answers to perplexing problems.

I do not know why these and other tragic things happen in our world. I do not have the answers. What I bring to the pulpit is the promise of God's presence and the certainty of God's care. "Even though I walk through the valley of the shadow of death," the psalmist said, "I will fear no evil, for you are with me" (23:4, NIV). What sustained the psalmist in the valley was not the knowledge of all the dimensions of the darkness. What strengthened him was the promise of God's presence. That is the central certainty that brings us boldly to the pulpit.

Need for Clarity

One of the seductive sins of preaching is overconcern with ourselves and how we are being received. Most of us like to be liked. I would much rather stand at the back door of the church after the service and have somebody say, "I really liked that sermon," than for someone to remark, "That was one of the worst sermons I have ever heard!"

We like to be well received. The problem is focusing on ourselves and on the question, "Will people like what I'm doing?" This often leads to a sacrifice of substance for style. The result may be ministerial competition that tries to decide, "Now who is the best preacher anyway?"

The test of good preaching can never be measured by the number of compliments we receive at the door. Good preaching is not decided by the ability to dazzle the congregation with the artistry of our words or the magnetism of our personalities. A strong test of good preaching is whether the message is presented clearly. That is the primary objective of our preaching. Do we present the message in such a way that it can be heard clearly so the Spirit of God can speak through it to the lives of our listeners?

I am especially convinced that clarity is important in the

times in which we speak. In moments of great complexity when people feel overwhelmed by the changes in life, they need to hear a clear word from the pulpit. In confusing times when we feel frustrated and depressed, we need to hear a clear word for the living of our days and our nights.

The prophet Jeremiah was ready to leave the preaching ministry when God spoke to him. Jeremiah was depressed. The prophet had preached as well as he knew how, and every time he gave the invitation, nobody came forward. He spoke with courage and conviction, but the nation would not listen to his message of repentance. Jeremiah was ready to give up and return his ordination papers to God. God told his prophet that it was time for him to hear a sermon. The first part of Jeremiah 18 is the sermon that God preached to His perplexed prophet and to a confused nation. The sermon is about a simple, familiar thing—the potter working at the clay. Through this picture of something that Jeremiah probably saw every day of his life, God reassured His preacher that life was still in God's hands. At times, life is difficult, and we do not understand everything that happens; but the clear message of the sermon was that God continues to form us, "shaping it [the pot] as seemed best to him" (v. 4, NIV).

In our own day when many people sit in the pews feeling confused in the face of life's complexities, preachers need to remember the power of clarity. Three things may help us in the process: focus, simplicity, and practicality.

First, we need to know what we want to say. I have preached sermons wanting to say too much or knowing I wanted to say something, but being unsure exactly what it was. That is why every sermon should have a clear, concise focus before we begin putting the sermon together. Otherwise, it is like wandering into the woods not remembering how we got in the middle of these tall trees and having no idea how we will get out. A sermon will not be clear to the hearer if it is not clear to the preacher. Before we set out on the journey of the sermon with the listeners, we need to know where we are headed and how we plan to get there.

Simplicity is also important in the creation of clarity. I will discuss the matter of simplicity in a later chapter on style, but I want to stress one aspect of simplicity here. Preachers should strive for simplicity in language. Theologically technical words should be avoided. Whenever possible, a word of one syllable should be used; and we should pay attention to the emotive, affective side of words. Generally, it is good to use a word that spurs some feeling in the listener or creates some image that she or he can attach to the idea.

Some may disagree about avoiding theologically technical language in a sermon. Some ministers argue that we need to educate lay people in the language and ideas that many of us were taught in our preparation as pastors. Ignorance is not bliss or blessed. Many of the lay people in our churches do hunger to know more and to go deeper in their study of the Bible. Alert pastors will provide teaching opportunities for their people to learn to ask questions, to discuss issues, and to make their judgments about important theological issues. Most of our lay people can understand and comprehend much more than ministers sometimes give them credit.

However, theological jargon should be avoided in the sermon. In most of our churches, people do not raise their hands and say, "I'm sorry I didn't get that." If we do use a technical word, we should explain it, although too much technical explanation results in sermons that sound pedantic. It becomes "show off and tell" time for the pastor.

Early one morning I went to the Emory University cafeteria to eat breakfast. At the next table were two medical students. I could tell they were medical students by their books and their conversation. They were discussing some illness whose name I did not recognize and cannot remember. One of them obviously knew more than his friend. He was trying to explain something about the varieties of this illness, and the student who did not know as much said, "I must have missed that explanation."

I had the strangest feeling. I have no idea what the

diagnosis was, but if I ever have that illness, I do not want to go to a physician who says, "I'm sorry. I missed class the day the professor was explaining that." I want my doctor to know! I want him or her to understand all the words, know all the technical language, and comprehend the concepts. But when my doctor explains it to me, I want it in words I can decipher.

As preachers, our task is to convey the message in ways that the congregation can hear. We take into account our listeners and the level at which they hear. A good rule of thumb is to keep the language simple and to try to give images to the ideas in our message.

In addition to simplicity, another important matter in creating clarity is practicality. Is the sermon practical? Does it say anything that relates to the lives of people? Does it have significance for those who listen? In a world of complexity and confusion, we want preaching that touches us where we live.

The preacher needs to be concerned about both the "what" and the "so what" of a biblical text. Conveying information about the Roman colony of Philippi is interesting to some people. It may even be necessary to give some sense of the text. At some point the minister needs to deal with the significance or the "so what" of the Scripture. "So what difference does that make to my life?" is a question most of us ask when listening to a sermon. Knowing about Philippi is worthwhile, but we really want to know what sustained Paul in the storms of life and why this prison epistle reverberates with the sound of joy instead of bitterness. How can we have that kind of peace and balance in our lives? What do we do when the circumstances of our lives seem overwhelming? How do we deal with disappointments and what does it mean to be "in Christ" in the crises and complexities of life? These questions beg for answers in our day and every day.

Preachers also need to be mindful that the gospel we proclaim both comforts and challenges. In the name of practicality, we want to avoid the kind of preaching that only binds up wounds. Sometimes the words of the Bible are intended to wound our indifference or apathy. The Bible has both tenderness and thunder, grace and judgment. Most people today want to follow a God who is big enough to help them face the problems of life. They want to be challenged by the vision of a Christ who, without apology, challenges them to follow Him.

Need for Community

When I went to teach at the seminary, I had to leave my family for several weeks. The most difficult times were eating by myself. One night I went to a place in Louisville that was famous for its hamburgers. I went through the line, gave my order and first name, and took a seat. When my hamburger was ready, a voice came over the loud-speaker, "Chuck, party of one." As I ate my hamburger alone that night I thought, "How do you have a party with one?"

The fact is that many people have a party of one at dinner almost every night. The church is facing many changes in society which will affect our preaching. The number of older adults, many of whom subsist alone, is growing. There is an increase in people experiencing the trauma of divorce and wondering if they still have a place in the church. Single-parent families and blended families are common today. The "sandwich generation" is caught between the needs of adolescent children and aging parents. Young people continue to turn to drink and drugs to ease their pain.

These are just a few of the changes that are taking place in our time. They have serious implications for preaching. For example, how do we structure a series of sermons on marriage and the family? At one time we assumed the "nuclear family" was our audience. Our messages were addressed to a father that worked, a mother who was a homemaker, and their 2.3 children, which was the average. In many churches today, the so-called nuclear family is a minority of the family units. Many families are made up of one. When I was a pastor in Florida, I remember the number of older people who lived alone. Some of them had retired to Florida with their spouses who had subsequently died. Now these single, elderly people found themselves separated from extended family.

Recently I was speaking with a woman who was a single parent. The church had always been a central part of her life. When her divorce came, it was devastating. She had dreamed of a long and happy marriage, but the dream had turned to ashes. "Where do I fit in with my church?" she asked me. At precisely the time in her life when she needed the closeness of a community, she felt alienated from the church. Preachers who approach a series of sermons on home, marriage, and the family exactly as they did twenty-five years ago will miss a great opportunity for ministry.

At the same time, we cannot ignore the concerns of nuclear families in the church. These families are also in great need. In all the churches I have been pastor, families have wanted help. The more traditional structures of family life also give rise to many stresses and strains.

Many homes resemble a "pit stop" where we race in to change for the next meeting or engagement. When my children were involved in church activities, music, soccer, baseball, swim lessons, and slumber parties, among other things, we threatened to replace the front door of our house with a revolving door. Our primary method of communication was a note on the door of the refrigerator. It is no wonder that a sense of isolation and alienation builds in many families. Mom and Dad seldom talk, and one day they are strangers to each other. Parents are busy, children are busy—the dog stands in the middle of the living room floor getting a crick in her neck from watching the parade of people pass in and out.

A great opportunity exists for preachers to be sensitive to the isolation within families and to preach on ways that a family can be a community. Families often settle for a quick prayer before the one weekly meal eaten together. Community can be fostered through the recovery of family devotions and mealtime. Churches that put emphasis on ministry to the family are finding positive response because families who live together want to know how to be "together."

Our preaching also needs to be sensitive to those who find their primary family in the church. Some have gone through a divorce. For many it is a shattering experience. The preacher does not begin the sermon by saying, "Divorce is now all right." Most people who have been through a divorce know the pain, the anger, and often the rejection they have experienced. They are usually the first to say that divorce is not all right because a dream dies, often leaving scars for the rest of their lives.

People do not want a minister whose attitude is "If it feels good do it," or "If the marriage doesn't feel good, then break it off." We need ideals and values. We want to know that some things are vitally important. We do not want the minister who performed our wedding whispering to us at the end, "Don't worry if your marriage doesn't make it." However, we do not live in the best of all possible worlds. Beautiful things get broken. We have watched our dreams become nightmares. The church is increasingly filled with those for whom a relationship has failed. More than anything at that moment, these people need to know that their relationship with God and the church is secure.

In our preaching, we need to make sure that people understand that the church is not just for those who make a fortune in business, win the beauty contest, or are state champions in the football play-offs. The church exists for everybody because we are brought into the community of faith not by our goodness but by God's grace and forgiveness. The Bible is clear: "All have sinned and fallen short of the glory of God" (Rom. 3:23, NIV). Our sins may be different, but we have all sinned. Our failures may be our own, but our faith is the same in Christ. The ground is level at the cross. When we come to Him, we come to each other. That is true community.

Need for Compassion

Most people seek to be loved, not so much for what they do but for who they are. I will always be indebted to a young banker named Bob Payne. Bob directed the Sunday night youth group at my home church in Miami, Florida. I will never forget his encouragement. I was a shy fifteen-year-old with little self-esteem. I saw very little positive in myself, but Bob took time with me, affirmed my gifts, and became the most significant human instrument in my call to the ministry. He related to me with compassion. He did more than say, "I care about you." He became involved in my life and invested himself in me. That is compassion. It is love in action.

The need for preaching that kind of compassionate love is tremendous. The population of our world is growing at an incredible rate, and the command to preach the gospel to all people has never been more imperative. How do we move people out of the church buildings to be the church in the world? How do we call people to care, not just about exurbia and suburbia, but about the growing urban areas of our world where the needs are staggering? How do we as preachers help people to develop the generosity of their lives and their resources to enable the gospel of Jesus Christ to be presented to all people? Preaching in the days ahead will demand a new vision of people who need the good news of Jesus and developing new strategies to reach them.

While we preach that God is seeking to reconcile each of us to Himself in Jesus Christ, we also need to be sensitive to the social needs of our time. In that striking judgment scene Jesus painted in Matthew 25, we are struck by the questions Jesus said the King will ask us. They involve our response to the hungry, the thirsty, the stranger, the naked, the sick, and those in prison. Does the church have anything to say about those issues? Is it all right to overeat and scrape food into the garbage disposal as long as we say that we love God? Can we praise God in our churches and then have the attitude that the person sleeping under the bridge could really make it in life if he applied himself?

I am not passing judgment on anybody else. Matthew 25

makes me uncomfortable because more often than not, I have not done "for one of the least of these" (Matt. 25:45, NIV). This message which judges us is part of the Bible. It is as inspired as John 3:16 or Psalm 23. Passages such as Matthew 25 should remind us that true preaching brings both comfort and challenge.

One experience I had made me aware of being sensitive to the needs of others and highlighted my own blindness to the pain of someone else. It was Mother's Day. I do not remember my sermon, but I am sure I was extolling the virtues of mothers. After the service, I was standing at the back door. As people came by, I saw out of the corner of my eye, a woman standing at the edge of the group. When everyone else had gone, she came over and spoke these words I shall never forget: "Pastor, more than anything I wish that I could be a mother." She spoke not with anger; she spoke with anguish. Then she turned and walked out of the church.

It dawned on me that afternoon that Mother's Day is the most painful Sunday for some in our church. I considered myself a caring pastor, but I had missed her anguish and that of many others. Since that time, I have never conducted a Mother's Day service where, either in the prayer or in the sermon, I did not remember those who more than anything else wish they had somebody to call them "Mother."

I tell that story to remind myself as a minister that compassion is not an easy thing. It requires sensitivity, sacrifice, and the selflessness to pour our lives into the lives of others. It is not easy; but, unless I am badly missing the mark, it is the good news we need to preach and to hear in these times...and in every time.

Exercises

I. Several times in his letters, the apostle Paul mentioned the things that he "knows," the certainties of his life. Look up *know* in a concordance; and after reading the texts, write a theme sentence for a sermon from each one.

II. Every sermon needs to have sense and significance, a "what" and a "so what." As preachers, we need to know what we want to say and we need to know that it has significance or importance to our listeners. After writing a theme sentence from the passages of Scripture expressing Paul's certainties, write a brief paragraph that makes the application to our lives today.

┌ 4 ┐

PREACHING
INSIDE WORSHIP

Most of the preaching we do takes place within the context of a worship service. Nothing we do in the church is more central or crucial than worship. Worship is realizing the "worth" of God. Out of that realization springs evangelism, education, missions, and all the church does. Without accepting the worth of God, we will not be motivated by any sermon to reach people who do not know the love of God in Jesus Christ. On the other hand, if we truly worship—if we have a sense of the gracious God who gives Himself to the world—nothing can stop us from sharing the good news.

In this chapter I want to focus on the place of preaching in the public worship service. This is not intended to be a theology of worship or a discussion of the elements in the order of worship. Excellent books such as Evelyn Underhill's, *Mysticism*, Geoffrey Wainwright's, *Doxology*, and Donald Hustad's, *Jubilate*, among others, deal in more detail with the why's and how's of worship. My concern is the role of preaching in the worship service. To understand the sermon's role in worship, we must examine briefly the two elements in most worship services that have great bearing on the way the sermon is seen: the invocation and the invitation.

The Invocation

At the beginning of the public worship service is "The Invocation and The Call To Worship." The basic question is,

"Who is being called to worship and whose presence is being invoked?" I have heard calls to worship that have begged, beseeched, pleaded, and prayed to God that He be present. The idea seemed to be that we had gathered for worship and were now inviting God to meet with us.

Is it God who needs to be called to worship? The Bible is filled with reminders of the presence of God. In that classic biblical passage on worship, Isaiah 6:1-8, the grieving prophet goes to the temple where God is already waiting to meet him. Isaiah needs to worship. He needs to find strength beyond himself and, in a world where people like the good King Uzziah die, Isaiah needs to find a God worthy of worship. The God who is worthy of His worship is already present with the prophet. Isaiah does not need to go looking for God or beg Him to come his way. God is there for Isaiah and more than anything wants to make His presence felt.

Our attitude as we enter the place of worship will affect both how we preach and how we are heard. Suppose as preachers we come to the sanctuary uncertain that God is even there. If God is there, we wonder if He wants to make His presence felt. Are we dealing with a God of revelation or a God of reluctance? Does God invite us to the church each Sunday; or do we invite God, waiting for Sunday to see if God accepts our invitation?

My own sense of worship and preaching has been energized by the conviction that it is God who invites us to worship God. What an exciting prospect that is! Some Sundays as a pastor I would come to preach, tired or distracted. The pressures of a busy week, the unanticipated crisis, the person who died unexpectedly, and the funeral service leave us emotionally limp. Those who preach on a regular basis know that there are Sundays when we come to preach, but do not feel like preaching.

Does the worship experience depend on our performance as a preacher? While legitimate disagreement exists about styles of worship, we must avoid the attitude that for worship to happen, we, as ministers, must make it happen. That puts enormous pressure on the preacher, but more than that, it is a heresy of the theology of worship. We come together because God calls us together. God is there to meet us and to make things happen. How I feel on a particular Sunday does not determine whether God will work in the lives of people. Worship does not ride on my frail shoulders. Whatever else worship is, it is the realization that we are dependent on God and not God on us. Therefore, when we enter the place of worship, we come because the God whose mercy and grace never change calls us and invokes us to meet Him.

The Invitation

How we view the invocation will affect our preaching. At the other end of many services is the "Invitation or the Call to Response." This is the moment in the service when the minister turns from the act of preaching to the congregation and asks, "Now, in the name of God, what will we do with what we have heard?"

Many religious traditions do not have an invitation in the service. People are not publicly invited to make a response at that moment. Some churches have ways of contacting a minister or the church to indicate that some decision has been made. Many of us, particularly in the Evangelical tradition, conclude our public worship services by singing a hymn and inviting people to walk down the aisle and share whatever decisions they have made.

The latter pattern of worship has strong precedent in the Isaiah 6 passage. Isaiah came to the temple burdened with grief. There the prophet encountered God. When he met God, Isaiah was confronted with his sin and, after confession, was forgiven. At this point the meeting of God and Isaiah took an unexpected turn. Isaiah did not leave the temple simply rejoicing in the forgiveness of his sins or grateful that God had given him grace sufficient for his grief. Instead, God called young Isaiah, "Whom shall I send? And who will go for us?" (v. 8, NIV). The moment of response changed Isaiah's life forever, "Here am I. Send me!" (v. 8, NIV).

Preaching Inside Worship

How does the invitation affect the way that we preach? It reminds those who preach that when we proclaim the Word, we recognize that it can change the lives of people. It is an awesome thought. Despite the jokes about people sleeping through the sermon, many people are listening for something that will make a difference. When Robert McCracken, a former pastor of Riverside Church in New York City, was asked why people keep coming to church, he replied somewhere, "They keep coming hoping to hear a word from beyond themselves."

The invitation is a reminder to me as a preacher that the sermon is more than a lecture, a "talk," a story with a moral, or a few nice words. The sermon is the vehicle through which the Spirit of God seeks to speak to the lives of people. Each Sunday the preacher faithfully tries to proclaim the Word of God. Who knows how God may move on a given Sunday? A woman hears her need for Jesus Christ and comes one morning to accept Him as the Lord for her life. A husband and wife, whose marriage is fractured almost beyond repair, come and rediscover a love that had seemed lost. A single parent listens for some word of acceptance and hears about the God in Christ who gives forgiveness for the past and freedom for the future.

The invitation is the part of the worship service for which we can never fully plan. We may plan the song we are going to sing. We may plan how we will receive people when they walk down the aisles. But we cannot plan how people will respond.

Those who preach should have in mind what they want the sermon to do. As Thomas Long reminds us in *The Witness of Preaching*, a sermon should have a function as well as a focus.[1] That is, the minister should decide whether the sermon is primarily intended to convert, to comfort, to encourage, or to do something else. The invitation should flow out of the intention of the sermon. Yet that does not limit the way that God may craft a message for the life of someone who is listening.

When I was a young minister, I often became irritated

when someone would tell me about something in the sermon he or she liked that I did not remember saying. I wondered if that person had been watching some television preacher earlier and had gotten our sermons confused. Neither was I happy if someone complimented me on what I thought was a minor part of the sermon. I wanted people to hear the "big stuff," the part I had spent the most time trying to shape.

The longer I preach the less insulted or irritated I become by those kinds of responses. Preachers learn to look for kind words, no matter how they come. More importantly, I realize we all listen to a sermon through the screen of our own situations. I have experienced it as a listener. On the way to making a big point, the preacher said something that became for me exactly the good news I needed to hear. As Gardner Taylor said, "How strange of God to make the uttered word, so fragile and so tenuous, the principal carrier of so precious a cargo as that incalculable love which he has intemporated and incarnated in Jesus Christ our Lord."[2]

We need to educate our congregations about the importance of the invitation. The tendency is to view the worship service as a spectator. Some people watch the performance of the choir and the pastor; when the performance is done, so is worship. The "show" is over; it's time to put on our coats and go home. In some churches people actually leave during the invitation. We need to recover the importance of the invitation. Worship is not complete until we have responded to God. We may not all go forward during the hymn of invitation, but some response is needed in all of our lives to this gracious God who gives Himself to us in Jesus Christ.

The Sermon

If the primary purpose of our worship is to lift people to God and remind them of God's worth, what then is the role of preaching in worship? What are we trying to do when we stand to preach? Preachers who stress evangelism will answer, "I am trying to preach so that people who do not know Jesus Christ in their lives will accept Him as their Savior and Lord." Evangelism is the pivot of their preaching. Other peachers may answer that they desire to see Christians nurtured or suffering people comforted. Some preachers may say that their fundamental focus is to call the church to become involved in the problems of the world.

All of these responses are legitimate concerns of preaching. The Bible speaks to individuals as well as to nations. It both comforts and challenges. We are called to come to know Jesus Christ as personal Savior, but also to follow Him as Lord. The preacher who calls people to know Christ but never calls them to be leaven in the loaf of our world is just as wrong as the preacher who calls people to the world without first calling them to Jesus as Savior and Lord.

In the ministry of Jesus, little division exists between calling people to Him and then calling them to be with Him as a presence in the world. Jesus was concerned about people whose spirits as well as their stomachs were hungry. He cared about the poor in spirit and the poor in substance. Jesus gave sight to those who were physically blind, but He also opened the eyes of those who were blind to life's most important lessons.

The preaching of Jesus cannot be reduced to an either/or formula; it is both/and. Likewise, our preaching needs to reflect that diversity of concern. Some preachers have a passion for evangelism. However, the call to Christ also needs to be a call to join Him in being an agent of reconciliation in our broken world. On the other hand, it is quite sad to see a minister who seems to have little or no conviction that people need to accept Jesus Christ in a personal way. These preachers may exhort people to make a difference in the world, but they overlook that to make a difference, people have to be different. That difference is made when Christ becomes the purpose and power for our living.

Preaching has different purposes; it does not have only one aim. However, most preachers have some guiding conviction about the purpose of preaching which helps to direct them in the selection of sermons. Within the context of worship, I want to suggest a purpose for preaching that may inform our approach to proclamation. My larger concern is that you and I approach the task of preaching with a sense of the size of our calling.

Isaiah 6 again provides the pattern. The prophet came to the temple defeated and discouraged. King Uzziah had died. We live in that kind of world: people die, dreams die, relationships die, plans die. As Isaiah looked at life around him, he saw the changes and knew that life could deal the unexpected. Where did Isaiah put the weight of his faith? If he had chosen to put it in the circumstances of life, he would have been overwhelmed. The good King had died. We ministers know what it is to deal with people for whom something or someone good is dying or has died.

Suddenly Isaiah was confronted with the living God. He saw the Lord seated on the throne, and above God were seraphim calling to each other. This is the vision of the eternal. In the world where kings die, there is another King who never dies. Where do we put the weight of our faith? Do we put it in the earthly—that changes and dies? Or do we put it in the eternal—that is constant and never dies?

Isaiah watched the vision, and then the prophet listened to the voices of the seraphim as they called out: "'Holy, holy, holy is the Lord Almighty; the whole earth is full of his glory'" (v. 3, NIV). In these words, I find the heart of preaching.

Preachers are called to lift the eyes of people to God. Some people who come to hear us carry heavy burdens, deep pains, intense struggles, and their own private suffering. That is all they can see. The preacher stands and dares to say, "Let's look for the eternal."

Some come to us indifferent. They come to church out of habit; it is the thing to do. These people are concerned about making it in life. Their eyes are on mortgage payments, college tuition, a demanding job. The preacher stands and dares to say, "Let's look for the eternal."

Some come spiritually satisfied. They look at their lives

which are better than most. They love God, if not with all of their heart, mind, and soul, at least with some of it. They like sermons that talk about positive thinking and how to be self-fulfilled; they look for a church that does not expect too much. And the preacher stands and dares to say, "Let's look for the eternal."

Some do not come at all. The church is insignificant to them. If pushed, some will profess faith in a kind of God, but this God has little relevance to their lives. The church is for those who need a crutch. Ministers are viewed as kindly, boring people who mean well but have little sense of what life is about. And the preacher stands and dares to say, "Let's look for the eternal."

Some come with gratitude, for life has been good to them. They have much for which to be thankful. And the preacher stands and says, "Let's look to the eternal and express our praise."

That day as Isaiah stood in the temple, the seraphim called out, "'Holy, holy, holy is the Lord Almighty; the whole earth is full of his glory.'" It was a reminder to Isaiah that God existed and was sufficient and sovereign. In the living of our days, it is easy to lose sight of God, particularly when the storms come. I have preached sermons in which I have dealt critically with Simon Peter for the night he took his eyes off Jesus, put his focus on the waves, and started to drown. It makes for a stirring sermon. "Why don't we keep our eyes on Jesus?" the preacher asks, and no one disagrees. We should all live that way. Storms come, but we keep our eyes on Jesus. The waves rise up, but we keep our eyes on Jesus. Difficulties pound our lives, but do we fear? No! We keep our eyes on Jesus.

Although that is the way we would like to live, it is not often the way I have lived. I can identify with the drowning, with feeling that the storm is too much, and realizing that I am too little. I can understand the grief of Isaiah. He came to the temple. Even in the throes of grief, Isaiah stumbled to the place of worship hoping to find some strength beyond himself. What do the seraphim do? They sing about a Lord who is almighty.

Preachers need to answer the questions: "What vision of God do I bring to the pulpit? What do I believe about God myself?" We stare into the faces of some people with problems far too big for any of our wit and wisdom. If we rely on our own cleverness, cuteness, or catchy phrase, we may draw attention to ourselves rather than to the God who changes lives. What Isaiah needed, what I need, and what all of us need is to come to the temple to meet the living God rather than to hear some clever priest with a gift for words. Therefore, we need to keep central in our mind that people have come, not to hear us, but to hear about and encounter the Almighty God who makes all the difference.

The seraphim also reminded Isaiah in the worship service that day that "the whole earth is full of his glory." It was a call to Isaiah to look again at life. When he looked at the world, he saw uncertainty. Uzziah had been good to the people, and the future seemed secure with his hand at the helm. However, the earthly king had died. What was going to happen now? The present was filled with grief, and the future was fraught with uncertainty. Isaiah longed for the "good old days."

We can all understand that uncertainty. When my daughter's fiance called my wife and me to ask if he could marry our daughter, we were happy. He is a wonderful young man. He seems to love our daughter deeply, and she loves him. They share important values. Although my wife and I were happy, why did we look as if the end of the world had come when we got off the telephone?

Diane and I did not sleep much that night. We were remembering. I retraced the past 21 years of our daughter's life. The day she was born, first day of school, riding a bicycle, her baptism, piano recitals, scraped knees, vacations, graduations—I remembered it all that night. I also knew the one thing I could not do was turn the calendar back. Life moves on. Things change. It was a new season in our lives, and we had to say good-bye to some things in order to say hello to others. The fear of change exists, however, because it is never easy to close one chapter even when starting the next one.

Uzziah was dead. The question for Isaiah was, "Is anything still certain?" The seraphim called Isaiah to see God's glory in all of life. Most of life involves change: we must say good-bye to certain things, and some things die. Today is not a duplicate of yesterday; we cannot anticipate all that tomorrow brings. The good news for Isaiah was that God was alive and at work in the world.

It is exciting to preach. Who else has the privilege of pointing to the Eternal in the midst of the earthly and calling people to faith in a God who is big enough for life and death? If we have done that, then, indeed, we have worshiped.

Exercises

I. When we come to the worship service, we come knowing that God is already present and present to us. Write an invocation expressing gratitude for God's presence and invoking the people of God to be present to God.

II. Look through several sermons you have preached and notice how you moved into the time of invitation. Do you feel a sense of expectation, or is it more a matter of routine? Are you as the preacher clear what you want the sermon to do in the lives of people so that your invitation fits the intention of the sermon? Does your sermon reach the climax at the end, or do you find that the last parts of your sermons tend to be anti-climatic?

Notes

1. Thomas G. Long, *The Witness of Preaching* (Louisville, Ky.: Westminster/John Knox Press, 1989), 78-91.

2. Gardner G. Taylor, *How Shall They Preach: The Lyman Beecher Lectures and Five Lenten Sermons* (Elgin, Ill.: Progressive Baptist Publishing House, 1977), 44.

PART II

PREACHING FROM INSIDE THE TEXT

⌐5⌐

GETTING INSIDE
THE TEXT

Pastors know the pressure of preparing sermons each week. For many of us, it involves more than a single Sunday morning sermon. Some ministers have preaching responsibilities for both Sunday mornings and Sunday nights, as well as a mid-week service. As a young Baptist minister said to me, "At our house we think every day is Sunday or Wednesday."

Whether it is once or several times a week, the process of preaching is demanding. It necessitates some kind of discipline on our part as preachers. We need a pattern that we can use to prepare our sermons so that we do not waste unnecessary time and energy each week developing a method of approach.

In preparing our sermons, most of us are eager to get something on paper. We want to have something to say even if we feel that it is not much to say. We are anxious to get an outline or a structure for the sermon. If we have not spent enough time in seeking a message, the costs in both time and enthusiasm will be apparent as we try to organize a sermon that lacks meaning to us.

Sermon preparation requires seeking something to say that has both sense and significance. There needs to be a clearly defined process. We need to have a word for people before we rush to organize how we will say it. Otherwise, we will be structuring "sound and fury signifying nothing" either for us or our listeners. In this chapter I want to discuss some important aspects in the process of moving inside a biblical text, sensing its meaning, and developing the message that we believe God wants us to speak.

Importance of a Biblical Text

An important trend in recent years has been a renewed emphasis on "biblical preaching." While that term means different things to different people, the important fact is that new attention is being given to the Bible in many pulpits. Several factors account for this renewed attention.

One such factor involves the issue of where does the authority of preaching rest? Does it rest largely in the role of the preacher? If so, then preaching can simply be our opinions or observations. However, while most people in the pews respect their preacher, they do not believe something simply because the minister says so. This raises the question, "Where is the authority of preaching?"

Many of us would say that authority rests in the Bible, the Word of God. While we may disagree on the words we use to describe our view of biblical inspiration, most will agree that the power to change the lives of people comes as the Spirit of God applies the Word of God to the lives of those who listen. The task of the preacher then is to hear that Word of God from the Bible and to speak it in ways that apply to those who hear.

Another factor in the renewal of biblical preaching is the hunger of people to know more about the Bible as it applies to their lives. Preachers cannot assume that people know the biblical stories or even the familiar passages from the Bible. I caution students about introducing the reading of the Scripture in a worship service with words like, "Most of you already know this story." Some people do not know the story. In addition to assuming too much, it immediately makes those who are not familiar with the text feel inferior.

Several years ago I attended a workshop at the College of Preachers in Washington, D.C. A part of our assignment was to preach a sermon and be critiqued by our preaching peers. Most of my group were from outside the southern

United States. In my sermon I alluded to the Old Testament story of Abraham, Sarah, and the birth of Isaac. I told it in such a way that I assumed the audience already knew the contours of the story.

When my sermon was evaluated, several people raised the question of whether the congregations where they preached would have understood my reference. It was a legitimate critique. Most of my preaching has been done in the South where I have assumed a certain level of biblical literacy. That assumption may need to be reevaluated. While many people hold the Bible in high esteem, they do not know its contents as well as we sometimes assume. People do seem to be hungry to know more of the Bible. They tend to go to churches where the minister is faithful to the Word of God and faithful to the needs of people.

While I make a plea for this renewed emphasis on "biblical preaching," we must consider what is meant by the term. Many of us would agree it is what we need, but we would disagree on what the term means. Some equate biblical preaching with expository preaching. These preachers define expository preaching as a verse by verse treatment of a segment of Scripture. It is an acceptable form of preaching, having great communicative power for some hearers. In fact, preaching is not viewed favorably by some people unless it takes this form.

My definition of biblical preaching is that the preacher takes seriously the biblical text for the sermon. It is the commitment by the preacher to move inside a text, to sense its meaning, to feel its texture, to experience its impact, and to communicate that meaning to the hearers. The form of the sermon may differ, but one thing is constant—the faithful study of a passage of Scripture so that when we preach, we are faithful to hear what it says and speak what we hear.

Ministers must select a biblical text and let it live in them so that it can later live in those who listen. How we select the biblical text will vary. Some ministers rely on the lectionary which provides various Scripture readings for each Sunday. The advantage of the lectionary is that it takes seriously the flow of the whole church year.

Others orient some of their preaching and text selection around pivotal seasons of the church year such as Easter and Christmas. On the other Sundays, they make their own selection of a biblical text. Where do we begin in choosing a Scripture for the sermon? Do we begin with the Bible, or do we begin with the needs of people and then go to the text?"

The choice is not always clear cut. The effective preacher lives both in the world of the Bible as well as in the world of people. As preachers, therefore, we are called to "exegete" or to get inside both worlds. If we choose to begin with a biblical text, we must discover its significance for our hearers. The words we speak may be true, but if they are unrelated to the lives of the people, they will have little impact.

If we begin with a human need we want to address, we must make our way to the biblical text as quickly as possible. At this point we need to be exceedingly careful. The temptation is to twist the text to make it say what we want. Most preachers have probably experienced this. Instead of listening to the Bible with openness, we bend its message to suit our agendas. That does not qualify as biblical preaching. In whatever way we select a text from which to preach, the commitment of biblical preaching is to listen as faithfully as we can to the Word of God and then preach it as clearly and as cogently as we can.

Hearing the Text

After selecting the biblical text, the preacher then reads it with prayerful listening. Most often when we think of preaching we think of the voice. The image we have of preaching is someone opening the mouth and beginning to speak. Behind the public image of preachers with their mouths open giving voice to the Word of God is the private image of the minister with ears and eyes wide open to the biblical text. Looking and listening precede effective speaking.

Unfortunately, many of us do not trust ourselves with the text. As a young pastor, I remember turning immediately to the commentaries to see what they had to say about the Scripture from which I was preaching. I felt intimidated by the text. Who was I to try to discern a word from God when the "biblical experts" were sitting on my bookshelves? Each week I would tell myself, "You are a grasshopper in a land of giants"; before I really encountered the text for myself, I wanted to see what the "giants" had to say.

My attitude robbed me of the adventure of meeting the text for myself and asking, "What does this say to me?" and, "What can it say through me to others?" I want to reclaim for myself and for those whom I teach the confidence in the leadership of the Spirit of God in reading the Bible. As a young person, I remember the confidence that we were given to read and to interpret the Bible for ourselves. That freedom and assurance made reading the Bible exciting. We listened and looked believing that God could speak to us through the Word.

I am not suggesting that we sell all of our commentaries, Bible dictionaries, word studies, and other helps. They are aids to us in understanding such things as the historical background of the text or the nuances of a particular word. This is no call for book burning or book bashing. As a preacher I want to have access to materials that give insight and information.

My concern is that we not begin with these helps. What no commentary can tell us is the particular situation in which we are preaching. An outsider cannot get inside my context. I come to the text with invaluable information. My question is not, "What does the text say?" but "What does the text say to the people to whom I will preach?" I will listen and look at the text with ears and eyes opened to the Word of God and to the world of my listeners.

How then shall we hear? I would make several suggestions about reading the text. *This precedes any work with outside helps* but assumes that, before preparing the sermon, we will spend time in checking the commentaries and other aids.

First, read the text with your *ears*. Read it out loud so that you not only see it but also hear it. The Bible is designed to be heard as well as read. It is not just a book with words on the printed page. It is an anthology alive with songs, poems, history, parables, letters, apocalyptic literature, and even genealogies. To read the letters of Paul and say, "This is just an epistle to be read with the eyes," is to miss much of the point. The letters of Paul were read to the churches, and they were received by the ears of the people.

Imagine what it must have felt like to have been a Christian in Philippi and to have heard the words of Paul:

> I thank my God every time I remember you. In all my prayers for all of you, I always pray with joy because of your partnership in the gospel from the first day until now, being confident of this, that he who began a good work in you will carry it on to completion until the day of Christ Jesus (Phil. 1:3-6, NIV).

Here was this little Philippian church with its own doctrinal difficulties and its own divisiveness. I am certain there were days when these Christians wondered what was going to happen to them. Then, as they gathered for worship, someone read the letter out loud; and they heard words that throbbed with assurance.

Picture yourself in one of the churches in the province of Galatia. The letter from Paul was read. After his rather formal introduction, he briskly said, "I am astonished that you are so quickly deserting the one who called you by the grace of Christ and are turning to a different gospel—which is really no gospel at all" (Gal. 1:6-7, NIV).

You listened both to what was said and to what was not said. Paul sounded angry. "I am astonished," the apostle said, causing those who listened to get the message. What is both said and unsaid in this letter is sadly revealing. The people in Galatia knew the structure of a typical letter in the first century. Letters almost always included a section of thanksgiving and gratitude for the recipients. Paul had this section in all of his other letters, but it is missing in Galatians. By putting ourselves in the role of the original hearers for just a moment, we are shocked by what we hear and by what we do not hear.

After reading the text with our ears, we need to read it with our *eyes*. I was in the home of a young couple whose daughter is not old enough to read, but she has already learned to love books. Her grandparents had given her a large picture Bible. As her parents and I were talking, she was sitting in the middle of the floor, turning the pages of the Bible and talking to herself about the pictures she saw. I enjoyed her sense of wonder and imagination. She showed excitement as she recalled bits and pieces of the biblical stories her parents had taught her.

I would like each of us to recover that childlike sense of wonder as we come to the Bible. Maybe we have traveled some of the roads too often. Maybe we preachers have handled holy things so often that they have lost their wonder to us. Perhaps we have learned to approach the Bible with the sole purpose of finding a message to preach, and in the process, have lost the excitement of being encountered by the Word.

Imagination is a powerful weapon in the arsenal of a preacher. It does not mean making things up or living in a fantasy land, twisting the text into distorted shapes. Rather, imagination is the power to see the story, to move inside its characters, to experience the emotions, as well as hear the words. Imagination gives height, depth, breadth, and length to words that are flat on the page.

Consider the parable of the prodigal son in Luke 15. The father went out of his house twice: first to welcome his younger son home and second to beg his older son to come home. This parable has all the elements of high drama. When the father went out to ask his older son to come to the party, he was met with a stinging reproach: "Look! All these years I've been slaving for you and never disobeyed your orders. Yet you never gave me even a young goat so I could celebrate with my friends" (v. 29, NIV).

Put yourself in the place of the older son. Imagine what it must have been like. You have been working all day out in the sun. When you come home, you find a party in honor of your brother who has probably never worked a full day in his life.

Luke puts an exclamation point after the older son's response, "Look!" I can understand his anger. On my best days, I would like to think that the appreciation and approval of others do not mean that much to me. I would like to think that I could go to a party and celebrate with anyone, even if I was not an honored guest. However, I know myself too well. I flinch when I hear what the older son said. It is as if someone held up a mirror in front of the way I often live. When I hear the story with my eyes, I see the people with red faces and clenched teeth, and I feel the rage and resentment.

My third suggestion is to hear the biblical Word with our *emotions*. It is imperative to think through a text and study it. We are called to love God with our minds, but we are also called to love Him with our hearts. We need to think through as well as feel through the biblical text which we are preaching.

For many of us, "feeling" the text may be the more difficult task. Our education trained most of us to think. As preachers, we come to the biblical text with the tools that we have acquired. We are usually asking, "What is the historical background; what is being said; who is saying it; what does this text mean?"

The emotional aspect of hearing a passage of Scripture is difficult for most preachers who are male: the feeling dimension of life makes some men uncomfortable. "Real men don't eat quiche"; they do not express feelings, especially ones like tenderness or sadness. These stereotypes make it more difficult for some of us to get inside certain texts and experience them.

Consider again the example of the parable of the prodigal son. The older son is enraged. He confronts his father outside the house. With phrases punctuated by exclamation marks, the son lashes out at his father for having the kind of love that will throw a party for a prodigal.

How does the father respond? How does he reply, not just at the level of words but at the level of feeling? "My son," the father said. The word used for *son* is a word that exudes tenderness. Jesus told this parable for more reasons than to illustrate one father's relationship to two children who had trouble coming home. It is the story of God and every person. Somewhere in these two sons we find something of ourselves.

Even more important than seeing ourselves, we find something profoundly true of the tender grace of God. To both of the boys, the invitation was the same—come home. Even at their worst moments, the sons were still his sons. That is amazing grace. God calls us whomever we are to come home and to claim our identity as God's children. For all of us, that is a message that should make us *think* and *feel* something. We experience that kind of love with both head and heart. As preachers, we listen to the text with our emotions.

We also listen with *empathy*. We need to find empathy with the people in the biblical story. One of the most dramatic scenes in the New Testament is the garden of Gethsemane on the night before Jesus was crucified. The Gospel of Luke powerfully portrays Jesus at prayer. For Luke, prayer is pivotally important in the life of Jesus and the life of His church. Before anything crucial happened, Jesus went to pray.

It is the night before His crucifixion. What did Jesus do? He prayed. Jesus took with Him three disciples and told them, "Pray that you will not fall into temptation" (Luke 22:40, NIV). What do these disciples do? Pray? No! They fall asleep!

When a preacher sees such a story, the sermonic juices flow. It seems perfectly designed for that Sunday when we want to exhort and admonish the church for falling asleep to the things of Jesus. The text seems to cry out, "Preach me!" What a passage to let the church know in no uncertain terms that it needs to pray more and pay attention to Jesus more.

However, Luke gave one piece of information that spoils this perfectly good sermon. Luke said the disciples fell asleep "exhausted from sorrow" (Luke 22:45, NIV). Now, I have a problem as a preacher.

Originally, I would have preached this sermon from the perspective of Jesus. I would have been Jesus; the church would have been the disciples; and I would have preached a sermon on commitment. "Why don't we stay awake to Jesus? Why don't we pray more?" The outline seemed to be there for the asking. If only Luke had said the disciples fell asleep because they were not committed enough, but that is not what Luke said. They fell asleep "exhausted from sorrow."

For just a moment, climb into the skins of the disciples and experience Gethsemane from their perspective. The reality of the death of Jesus was sinking in. They had tried to deny and even to stop Jesus from talking about it. These were the men who had left everything a few years before to follow Jesus. They hardly knew Jesus, much less understood His dream for them, but they had followed. They listened to His sermons, watched Him heal people, heard His message of hope, and came to put their trust in Him. Now, in a few hours, the Giver of that dream and hope would die in a savage way.

What do you and I do when life seems to lose its purpose? How do we respond when the dark clouds roll in and we wonder if we will ever see the sun again? Where do we go when the dream seems to die? There have been days when I have wanted to pull the cover over my head and go back to sleep. We have experienced those moments when deep disappointment sapped our energy; all of our strength was needed just to stay on our feet.

Luke said the disciples fell asleep, not because they were

bad, but because they were sad. This passage of Scripture is not about the deliberate indifference of disciples to Jesus. It has little to do with lack of commitment. It has much to do with the kind of despair that washes over us when life seems to make no sense; all we want to do is get away from the pain.

Jesus did ask His disciples, "Why are you sleeping?" Then He told them once more, "Get up and pray so that you will not fall into temptation" (Luke 22:46, NIV). What is the message of these words? In the Gospel of Luke, prayer for Jesus was a way of sensing God's presence and providence in the most perplexing times. Prayer was the way that Jesus found strength from God to face whatever was ahead.

That is His message for disciples who are overwhelmed. What we need is the same thing that Jesus needed— strength from beyond ourselves. The answer to the cruel crises of life is not to withdraw more into the tight circle of our grief but to reach out in prayer to the God of hope.

Empathy with persons portrayed in the Bible is important for those who preach. Another shape empathy takes that is vital for preaching is an understanding of those to whom we preach. To whom do I speak? What are their ages, their sex, their hopes, their fears, their dreams, their nightmares? Do I serve a fairly young congregation filled with people who are trying to make it big in life? Am I speaking to people who live in big houses but who are never at home with themselves? Do I find many in the middle years of life, at the height of their personal power, but reassessing whether the journey has been worth it? Are there many elderly people in my church? Some of them believe they have nothing more to give and therefore are no longer worth anything. They know that death is not far away. How do I preach to them so that they will have courage to face the living of their days and assurance that, if they are in Christ, death is not a dead end but a doorway to eternity?

When preachers move inside the biblical text, they do not take the trip by themselves. They bring people with them asking, "What does this say to me?" The minister who hears the text effectively will never be accused of preaching sermons that do not touch the places where people live, move, and have their being.

The Sense and Significance of the Text

After hearing the text, the preacher is now ready to move to the commentaries and other helps. At this point in the process, some ministers spend an unnecessary amount of time. Be selective in the use of commentaries. For example, if I am preaching from the Book of Psalms, I do not have time to read everything. If I try, it will paralyze my preparation. Preachers need to overcome the feeling that the next book will have a new insight. We simply do not have the time to read everything. Good choice of commentaries and other aids is the key.

Next, we are ready to state the theme of our sermon in one, clear, positive sentence. What is it that I want to say? I need to know my purpose before I begin to structure the sermon itself. I want to speak the message I have chosen to preach in a way that will be clear to me and will guide the organization of the sermon. I am trying to create order out of what has been some chaos. Reading the text, praying over it, thinking through it, trying to feel its impact, writing down impressions and ideas involve some chaos. Being uncomfortable with chaos, we sometimes rush to impose a structure on a biblical text we have not really heard.

Initially, hear the text and make note of anything that comes to mind. Order will begin to emerge out of the chaos. As a preacher, I begin to see the message I want to preach. I check the commentaries to see what they have to add to the theme developing in my mind. I now want to write the guiding theme of the sermon in a sentence to help me clearly understand what I am trying to let God say through me in the sermon.

The temptation exists to try to say too much in one sermon. When we do that, we often wind up diluting the things we really want to say. As I develop the theme of the sermon, I have to say no to some important ideas, knowing that I will say yes to them at a later time.

We may call this process getting the *sense* of the text. What do I want to say through this particular passage of Scripture? What is my point? What is the focus? What is the central theme? What is the big idea? What is the sense of the text? Before you start to prepare what you have to say, be sure that you know clearly the focus of what you want to say.

At this stage of sermon preparation, it is important to know the *significance* of the text and the message. The preacher asks: Is my message really important? Some sermons die in the place of worship not because their content is untrue, but because the message has little significance. I heard a radio preacher speak on the theme, "Jesus was a celestial Being with a celestial body." When he had finished his sermon, he announced that the next day he would continue the same theme. The preacher may have had some listeners who were touched by his sermon. I have to commend him for his passion for what he was preaching: his passion came through the radio. But I commented to my family as we were traveling on vacation, "I don't get it."

I missed the significance. The preacher's message may have been true. Frankly, I was a little confused about the content. I did know the sermon did not come within a hundred miles of my needs. Driving down the highway that day, I was none the better for having heard, "Jesus was a celestial Being with a celestial body."

If we enter the pulpit with the conviction that the message is clear and has importance both to us and to our listeners, we will speak with deeper insight and greater power. The people in the pew will know that we have had something to say that makes a difference. Before I begin to put structure to my sermon, I need to know both the sense and the significance of the message, both the what and the so what. Then as I prepare the message and deliver the sermon, I will be undergirded by the firm belief that what I preach is true to the Word of God and true to the lives of the listeners.

Exercises

I. It is interesting to hear different "voices" read a Scripture text. Ask a group of people in your church to study a particular text on which you are planning to preach. Have them come together and each one read the passage. Then have the members of the group talk about what they "heard" that they had not heard before.

II. Read Psalm 23. Go back through the words and note each verb that is used. Think about the verbs, and try to "feel" their impact on your life.

III. The next time you prepare a sermon, think especially about the significance of it. Why is this important? What difference do you believe hearing this message can make in the lives of people? Is what you want to say both true and important to you as well as to those to whom you speak?

6

CONNECTING THE TEXT
TO THE LISTENERS

The preparation of a sermon has two distinct phases. The first phase is getting the message, which involves much of what was discussed in the last chapter. The minister selects the biblical text, encounters the text, works with commentaries and other aids, and develops both the sense and the significance of the sermon. Before moving out of the first phase of preparation, the preacher should know clearly the "what" and the "so what" of the message. These questions should have been answered: What do I want to say and why is this important?

In the second phase, the preacher is ready to put structure to the sermon and connect the text to the listener. We need to remind ourselves that the primary purpose of preaching is to communicate a message to people. The true test of the form of a sermon is clarity, not cleverness. Our chief purpose in preaching is to make the message clear.

The Who of the Sermon

Many years ago Phillips Brooks coined what is probably the most enduring definition of preaching as "Truth through Personality." Brooks saw truth and personality as the essential elements in preaching. On the one hand, the preacher deals with truth, which according to Brooks is "universal and invariable."[1] At the same time, that truth in preaching comes through a person who is "...special and always different."[2] Brooks encouraged ministers to recognize their own individuality and not to be afraid to let their own personhood be known in preaching.

A balance needs to be maintained between truth and personality. If truth is emphasized to the exclusion of personality, preaching can become sterile. However, if personality overshadows truth, the result is the kind of proclamation in which the medium becomes the message. The gospel does not ride on the personality of any of us. It will keep us humble to realize that the kingdom can go on even without our presence.

However, we need to recognize that the biblical text is connected to the listeners *through* the person of the preacher. Who we are affects what we say and the way we say it. The Word of God does not travel to the lives of listeners untouched by the person who proclaims it. The preacher is a part of the message, as the sermon does not come *around* us but *through* us to people. We need to examine self-discovery and self-disclosure as they relate to the message we proclaim.

Self-discovery

From the beginning stages of preparation through the delivery of the sermon, preachers should be involved in hearing the word for their own lives. I have learned to dislike the phrase, "getting up a sermon." It suggests that we can go to the Word of God without any involvement on our part. The image emerges of a minister detached from the sermon and trying to shape something in which there is no personal investment.

In his outstanding book, *The Recovery of Preaching*, Henry Mitchell emphasizes the note of celebration that is found in most black preachers. Mitchell states:

> The story must be internalized in the preacher, peopled by characters he has known for years and for whom he has such deep feelings that he can authentically recreate the action and communicate the experience. A kind of saturation is required.[3]

How we approach preaching is largely determined by what we want to happen in the people who listen. If our goal is simply to communicate information, we can handle the text without letting it touch us. I can give the historical background of a passage of Scripture without any real investment of myself.

However, if the desire of my preaching is to have people "experience" the truth of the text, I must stand in front of its message and feel the impact. I must live with the Word and pray that somehow the Word will live in me and through me. As Mitchell says, "a kind of saturation is required."

While this is demanding for any preacher, it is essential in maintaining excitement in our preaching. Preparing as well as preaching sermons can become tedious and boring if we are designing and delivering a message that we have not first heard ourselves. If we come to our preparation and preaching with the sense that we, as preachers, may encounter the God we proclaim in a fresh way, it brings new vitality to our proclamation.

I remember well a moment of self-discovery that has sustained me in some difficult days. When our son David was going through a series of radiation treatments, he became quite ill. I preached a series of sermons on Psalm 23. I have found that in the most trying times of my life, I move toward the familiar biblical texts. No matter how many times I have heard them, I do not grow weary of those words of reassurance.

The text for this particular Sunday morning was Psalm 23:4. Because most of us have learned the words in the King James Version, I was using that translation: "Yea, though I walk through the valley of the shadow of death, I will fear no evil: for thou art with me; thy rod and thy staff they comfort me." The danger with a familiar passage of Scripture is the assumption that we have heard all there is to hear. However, as I read again these words, I was suddenly captured by the power of the phrase, "For thou art with me."

Just five words, but on that day I discovered them in a new way.

The psalmist was moving through a valley. What sustained him? Did he understand the reasons for the difficult days? Did he give explanations for the dimensions of darkness? Not at all! What sustained and strengthened the psalmist was the assurance of the presence of God, "For thou art with me."

So many times through the illness of our son I had asked, "Why our family?" I still do not have answers to the why question and am sure I will never fully understand in this life. What I did have, though, was the reassurance of God's presence. That Sunday when I came to preach, it was like sharing fresh water from which I was also drinking.

Not every sermon has that kind of impact on us. I came that week with some unique needs; my own woundedness had opened me to hear something that I desperately needed to know. The principle is still the same for all of our sermons: we pray to be encountered by the Word of God so that as we hear it, prepare the message, and preach the sermon, we have the freshness of our own discovery of new depths.

Self-disclosure

Self-disclosure is the cause of much debate among teachers of preaching. Some feel that any references to the preacher draw away from the attention that should be on Christ. The words of Paul to the Corinthians, "but we preach Christ crucified" (1 Cor. 1:23, NIV), are usually cited as evidence. While none of us would disagree with Paul that Jesus Christ is the focus of preaching, we are aware that Paul sometimes referred to his own experiences to illustrate his point.

Self-disclosure can be overdone. I know of one minister who constantly refers to his beautiful wife and his wonderful children. I have never met this minister's family so I will take his word on it. However, people who listen to him faithfully get weary of the perfection and probably a little suspicious that everything is as blissful as portrayed. I know at my own house we would not want to invite the members of the church to drop in anytime to see if everything was beautiful and wonderful.

At the other extreme is the minister who discloses more than the congregation is able to handle emotionally. Another minister shared in a sermon the severe depression he had been experiencing, his contemplated suicide, and his marriage that might not survive. The congregation was overwhelmed. Many felt great sympathy for their pastor, but they hardly knew how to respond. Ministers do get depressed, some even suicidal. Our marriages are not immune from the stresses of life. The strain on the family of the pastor may be greater because of expectations and visibility. However, when we disclose something from the pulpit, we need to ask ourselves if the people can handle it. Seeking professional help may be our best route rather than using the pulpit as a place for our personal catharsis.

Self-disclosure needs to be used as a way of reinforcing the truth we are sharing. If the disclosure is designed to gain pity or sympathy for the minister, then it should be avoided. That kind of emphasis on oneself is not the point of preaching.

Preachers need to consider whether people can identify with what is being shared. When I tell the story of our son David, I realize there are probably only a few people in the congregation whose families have had experiences with brain tumors. However, most people have had disappointments in their lives or dreams dashed that have caused them to pause in the frantic rush of life and ask, "What is really important?" When preachers disclose something of themselves, they need to connect with the lives of the people who hear.

Self-disclosure does not have to be serious. Important truths can be shared through the humorous. I have often told the story of Bill Smith. Christina and Bill were members of the small country church in southern Indiana where I was pastor while a student in seminary. Bill was in his early 80's, a crusty old farmer whose favorite pastime was watching wrestling on television. One Sunday afternoon I stopped by to visit Bill. Christina directed me to the back room of the old farm house where Bill was watching "Championship Wrestling." I pulled up a chair next to him, but he could not have cared less about my presence. Bill was involved body, mind, and spirit in the wrestling. What I said that afternoon has to be one of the worst mistakes of my ministry. Maybe I was angry that Bill was not paying any attention to me; maybe I was tired that afternoon. I looked at Bill and said, "You know that wrestling is not real." If I could have retrieved those words from the air, I would have swallowed every one of them.

I will never forget the way that Bill Smith looked at me that Sunday afternoon. It was not the anger I expected. Rather, it was disappointment—profound disappointment that as his pastor I had not taken seriously that which he took very seriously. I will long remember the expression on Bill's face. It has taught me to be gentle with things that people take as important. I share this story with the students in my seminary classes knowing that some will want to change the people in their churches by sundown of the second day they are there.

The What of the Sermon

Most of my ministry has been as the pastor of a local church. In 1989, I was invited to be a professor of preaching at The Southern Baptist Theological Seminary. While I have since served twice as interim pastor, most of my preaching has been done in a different church almost every Sunday. Since becoming a teacher of preaching, I have often remarked that the best preaching is done by the pastor of the church.

That does not mean that the pastor is always the most eloquent or gifted preacher, although many pastors I know are both. Those of us who come for a short stay bring a different voice, as well as what we believe to be our best sermons. When the preaching series, the revival, or the Bible study is finished, we pack our bags and leave town.

The pastor remains, living and experiencing life from the perspective of the people. Good pastors are observant. They listen. They look. They walk with church members through their joys and through their griefs. When they stand to preach, they are heard, not just as the preacher for the day, but as the preacher who as pastor loves them and cares for them.

A good preacher explains and interprets both the Word of God and the world of the hearers. Proclamation without the authority of the Bible is impotent; preaching without a connection to the lives of people is irrelevant. Both impotency and irrelevance are deadly sins of the pulpit. What we say needs to be true, especially as it relates to the lives of people.

Careful hearing, or what Leander Keck calls "priestly listening,"[4] is important for the preacher. When we read a biblical text to seek a message, we need to go with the questions, the hopes, the fears, the faith, and the struggles of the congregation. Pastors must have ears open as they move among the people, listening to the things that are unsaid as well as said.

It is important to listen to all parts of a congregation. Ministers who spend all of their time with just the people their own age or those who live in their neighborhood will miss the varied voices that are a part of any church. When I was pastor, I would never miss Vacation Bible School because of the lessons the children taught me. I know some pastors who schedule their vacations that week, but I can remember some wonderful experiences with the children.

One year our church held the joint worship service at which all of the children gathered at the end of the morning. I was getting hungry, and I picked up a peppermint from my secretary's desk and put it in my mouth. When I reached the sanctuary, I sat on the front row next to a little girl with bright eyes and bouncy curls. After a moment, she looked up at me and said, "I smell peppermint." I was feeling bad because I did not have one to offer her. But she was not finished. Looking up at me just as seriously as she could, she said, "My dad doesn't let me have candy in church." I limped out of the sanctuary that day and have never taken another piece of candy into a worship service. Just think! I would have missed her lesson had I not been sitting next to a child, eager to let me know my behavior was not acceptable.

I also recall visiting a man in a nursing home. He was a prominent attorney who had suffered a stroke, paralyzing one side of his face. I bent down by the bed but could not understand anything he tried to say. For a few minutes I found myself overwhelmed with fear. Here was a person who lived by the power of his words, and now he could not speak. I thought to myself, "What if something like this should happen to me?" I take for granted the çapacity to speak. I spend much of my time shaping words that I assume I will be able to say. But what happens if your voice is reduced to a faint mumble and even the person bending over your bed cannot comprehend the meaning?

I talked to this man for a few minutes, said a prayer, held his hand, and then got ready to leave. I noticed on the wall a card from his wife. It was there for everyone to see, and she had written, "To my dearest husband whom I love with all of my heart."

It is difficult to describe the feeling I had at that moment. It was like being enveloped by an overwhelming sense of grace. What this wife was saying to her husband is that I love you for who you are, not for what you do. She loved him as her husband with all of her heart, and her love was not contingent on anything that he could or could not do.

Perhaps, the reason that moment held such power for me is that I struggle to accept the fact that anyone, including God, can love me for who I am. I have always feared failure because it meant that people would stop loving me. For all of my preaching about the amazing grace of God, I have had enormous difficulty accepting it. That evening in the nursing home was a breakthrough for me. What if I had not gone? I would have missed the power in the words of a loving, accepting wife.

What makes the preaching of a pastor so potentially powerful is that the speaking grows out of pastoral listening. The sensitive pastor knows the questions within the congregation and brings to the text what nobody else can—people who are known. The "what" of the sermon is shaped by the interaction of Scripture, pastor, and people; the result is a sermon that speaks to particular persons with particular needs.

For the more itinerant preacher who does not preach in a pastoral context, two things have been helpful to me. First, I try to determine as much as possible about the situation through the eyes of the pastor. Second, I have been helped by the concept of "shared story."[5]

Whenever I preach, no matter where it is, I enter the pulpit with a fundamental assumption that underlies my proclamation: all people need the revelation of God in Jesus Christ. This assumption is "shared story." We may not have walked through the doors of the church building that Sunday saying, "I'm here because I need God." We may not have thought much about it. However, no matter what our differences, we have one thing in common: we need to know God. Our universal exigency helps me keep in focus that the reason above every other for preaching is to allow God to be known through the words we speak.

The How of the Sermon

Much recent study in the area of homiletics has dealt with the form or structure of the sermon. After we have moved inside the text and have developed the sense and significance of the sermon, we must ask, "How do we say this in such a way that the message is heard?"

We are moving the sermon from the study to the sanctuary. How we do this is vital to the success of the sermon. In the study, the preacher may have excellent insights, but if that minister is not able to communicate them, the sermon loses its impact. The sermon must be heard; how we organize or structure the sermon will be a major factor in how well the words are received by the listener. In determining the form of the sermon, several factors are important.

One factor to be considered is the way that people *listen*. A number of years ago I preached at a small fishing village off the southwest coast of Florida. Most of the people that I met were "down-to-earth, no-nonsense" kind of people. I was preaching one night on the miracle when Jesus multiplied the loaves and fish into a meal for the multitude. The text was from the Gospel of John, which mentions the boy who brought his meal from home. Trying to update the story, I said that he had his loaves and fish in a brown bag. Immediately, someone in the congregation said in a voice that could be heard throughout the church, "They didn't have brown bags back then!" I made no further effort that weekend to contemporize the biblical story. People listen in different ways. A good preacher becomes aware of how people listen and what ways are most effective in communicating with them.

A second factor affecting the structure of the sermon is the *purpose* in preaching the sermon. We need to know both what we want the sermon to say and what we want it to do in the lives of the listeners. Let's suppose that I am preaching a sermon intended to teach. I am speaking to a congregation confused about an issue and am sharing information I hope will help in dealing with the difficulty. With that as my purpose, I will spell out very clearly what I want to say, and at the conclusion of the sermon I will reiterate the major point of the message.

Another occasion in which I might use this approach is a funeral sermon. In a time of grief, we want to hear a clear word of hope. This is not the time to see how clever or creative I can be, because people will not have the capacity to follow a sermon that demands a lot of careful listening.

On the other hand, if I am preaching a sermon which may generate some resistance, I may not want to unveil my theme until the end of the sermon. The "inductive" style is useful when the preacher is trying to get people to take the trip and arrive at the same destination. If I announce my destination at the outset, the people may not want to go there. Most of them will get off the train, and I will have arrived alone.

One other matter that may influence the purpose of a sermon involves those occasions when we are speaking to an unfamiliar congregation. When I am preaching to such a congregation, I deliberately choose a biblical text that I believe has some familiarity to most people. Hopefully, our common understanding establishes a bond between the hearers and me. While we do not know each other, our looking at a passage of Scripture allows us to give a nod of recognition.

A third factor to consider in the structuring of the sermon is the biblical text from which we are preaching. What is the *structure* or *literary genre* of the Scripture? Is it history, a poem, a hymn, a letter? What form does the text have?

Recent books on the literary forms of the Bible are reminding us that the form of the text should have an impact on our preaching. Thomas Long, professor of preaching at Princeton Theological Seminary, has written an excellent book, *The Literary Forms of the Bible* (Westminster Press). Long reminds us that we need to take seriously both the shape of a text as well as its substance.

The tendency of preachers has been to treat all biblical texts the same. The preacher goes to the passage of Scripture to try to extract the points. Doing so has often denied our hearers the opportunity to "experience" the text for themselves. Black preaching has through the years taught us the power of the experience of a story. The biblical story was retold imaginatively by the preacher, and the people who heard became participants in the story instead of mere spectators.

A black minister preached a sermon about the lost sheep described in the story of Jesus. With great patience, he told about the one lost sheep as it "nibbled" its way little by little from the other sheep. I was listening, but I was also in the story. This minister took seriously the form of the biblical text and allowed the story to become our story.

Contrast that with the preacher who reads the same text but begins the sermon, "This morning I have three points." What we will miss in this sermon is the experience. We may leave the church with some information the preacher has distilled for us, but we will not get the "feeling" which is such a powerful part of any good story.

In shaping the sermon, one final factor of great importance has occasionally been overlooked. I am referring to the gifts and personality of the preacher. We each need to grow and to expand the range of our competency; but if we try to adopt a style incompatible with who we are, the result can be disastrous.

One way to structure a sermon is termed "expository preaching." Frequently, this term is too narrowly defined. To many people, expository preaching is a verse by verse examination of a text, often using an alliterative outline.

Expository preaching, or the "exposition" of a biblical text, has much to commend it. It takes the message of the Bible seriously. Unless the outline is so strained that we wonder if the minister spent more time with a thesaurus than the text, expository preaching can be an effective way to have people remember the message.

Preachers who structure their sermons this way tend to be propositional and want things stated as clearly and as cleanly as possible. If illustrations or stories are used, they serve to illuminate some stated truth.

Expository preaching need not be taught as the only biblical way to preach. Jesus employed various styles in preaching. The Sermon on the Mount in chapters 5—7 of Matthew is, for the most part, straightforward, clean, and clear.

> Do not store up for yourselves treasures on earth, where moth and rust destroy, and where thieves break in and steal. But store up for yourselves treasures in heaven, where moth and rust do not destroy, and where thieves do

not break in and steal. For where your treasure is, there your heart will be also (Matt. 6:19-21, NIV).

Jesus issued a clear challenge, leaving little for the imagination.

A second example of a way to structure sermons is the "narrative" approach. Like "expository preaching," "narrative preaching" is subject to a wide variety of definitions. I am referring to the sermon that tells a story or a succession of stories with little interpretative material.

Consider the parables. At the end of the parable of the prodigal son, Jesus did not tell us whether the older brother went home with the father. If I had been one of the disciples, I would have raised my hand and asked Jesus to finish the story. However, ambiguity may be there on purpose. Perhaps, Jesus was saying that each of us is the one who finishes the story and decides whether to go home.

As a teacher of preaching, I want to honor the God-given personalities and gifts of my students. Some students can put together exceptionally fine expository sermons. Others move through the biblical text, recreating the experience. Although we do not leave class with five points, we leave with a sense of the closeness of God.

Biblical preaching takes a number of shapes; there is no one way to do it. It is important to take seriously the Scripture passage from which we preach and to keep in mind that our task is to communicate the message. We may decide to use different strategies but are thankful for the diversity of people God has called to the ministry of preaching.

Exercises

I. Before we can preach a text, we need to hear it for our own lives. Read carefully Psalm 23. Write down the ways that you find the message of the shepherd psalm speaking to your life.

II. Think of an experience from your own life that has had

great meaning for you. How could other people relate to your story and what you have learned?

III. Take a few minutes at the end of what you consider an "ordinary day" to remember and reflect. Write down something that has happened or been said to you. Why do you remember it? What about that experience may help you as a minister to understand more about the needs of people?

IV. Suppose you are the pastor of a church dealing with a difficult or controversial issue. After you have selected a biblical text, think about the development of a sermon that will help lead them to see the truth you want to communicate.

Notes

1. Phillips Brooks, *On Preaching* (New York: The Seabury Press, 1964), 14.

2. Ibid.

3. Henry Mitchell, *The Recovery of Preaching* (San Francisco: Harper and Row, Publishers, 1977), 37.

4. Leander Keck, *The Bible in the Pulpit: The Renewal of Biblical Preaching* (Nashville: Abingdon, 1978), 53.

5. Morris J. Niedenthal and Charles L. Rice, "Preaching as Shared Story," in *Preaching the Story,* ed. Edmund A. Steimle, Morris J. Niedenthal and Charles L. Rice (Philadelphia: Fortress Press, 1980), 13.

┌ 7 ┐

GETTING INTO
AND OUT OF
THE SERMON

How do you begin a sermon, and how do you end a sermon? We are familiar with the sermon that has excellent content. The preacher obviously has spent a lot of time in discerning an important message to speak and shaping that message into a sermon. What was missing was a good introduction. By the time the minister got to the body of the sermon, the congregation was checking their watches or wondering what the next week held.

At the same time, we have experienced sermons whose impact was greatly diminished because the minister did not have an effective conclusion. Few things will damage the effectiveness of a sermon more than not knowing *how* or *when* to end. This is particularly true for those whose services each Sunday lead into a hymn of invitation or commitment. We need to be aware of our purpose in the sermon and be able to bring our listeners to a point of decision. In this chapter we will discuss matters pertaining to getting into and out of the sermon.

The Introduction

Establishes a Relationship

The introduction establishes a relationship between the preacher and the listeners. Preachers should realize that how they look and act before getting up to preach has a profound impact on the way people listen.

Let me give two negative examples of what I mean. Several years ago I went to hear a minister preach. The service was supposed to begin at 11 a.m. It was five minutes after the hour before the choir and pastor appeared. I watched him as he came through the door and took his seat in front of the congregation.

He looked as if church were the last place he wanted to be that morning. He shuffled into the sanctuary with his head down, slouched in the chair, and never changed his somber expression. By the time he came to preach, I expected nothing and got exactly that. This minister began the sermon in the same way he had entered the sanctuary. There was no excitement, no anticipation, no sense of worship, all of which was reflected in the attitude of the congregation.

The second example is a minister who has an outstanding preaching reputation. On the Sunday I heard him, I was impressed by his obvious gifts and skills. However, I found myself having to overcome a major barrier in hearing him. During the service prior to the sermon, he paced around the chair where he was standing, did not take part in the singing of the hymns, paid no attention to anyone else who had leadership in the service, and kept his eyes opened during the prayer (yes, I peeked). His attitude seemed to be, "Let's get all the rest of this over with so I can get to the pulpit." I wondered if he realized what he was communicating to the congregation by his behavior. If I were watching him Sunday after Sunday, I would draw the conclusion that nothing mattered in the worship service except the sermon.

People are listening to more than just our words. When I come to a worship service as the preacher, I need to have a genuine sense of excitement and anticipation. No matter how I feel on a particular Sunday, people have come to worship God; and He may make an impact on the life of some person there.

When we come to the pulpit, we need to come with a tone of confidence. The word *confidence* literally means "filled with faith." The confidence we have is not in ourselves or in our words but in God who chooses the foolishness of preaching to do incredible things. Therefore, as a preacher I need to keep in mind that the introduction to the sermon is more than the first words I speak. It is also the attitude and demeanor I bring to the entire service of worship.

Makes a Promise

The introduction should make a promise that the rest of the sermon keeps. The promise is most often made implicitly or indirectly by the preacher. In some situations ministers state very clearly in the introduction what they want to say, but usually the promise is more indirect and implicit.

For example, a preacher chooses as the text the story of the day that Jesus multiplied the loaves and fish into a meal for the multitude. Suppose the theme for the sermon is, "Despite our differences, the one common bond for all people is our need for Jesus Christ." The preacher begins the sermon with the text itself and makes the point that out of all the miracles of Jesus, this is the only one recorded in each of the Gospels. The question is raised, "Why?" Why is the day that Jesus multiplied the loaves and fish on the green Galilean hillside remembered by Matthew, Mark, Luke, and John?

Could it be that this mighty act was remembered so vividly because it was a reminder to the early church that we all have two kinds of hunger? One hunger is fed by physical bread; the other hunger is for something to fill a world of emptiness. This hunger is fed by Jesus as the Bread of life. The sermon would develop around the one need that we all have and the one way that need can be met. The introduction indirectly promised an explanation for the significance of Jesus' miracle.

Several things need to be kept in mind in remembering the promissory note of the introduction. What we promise should be something that people want or need for their lives. Our sermon may be dealing with a truth, but it must have significance for the lives of the hearers. If what we promise is too abstract or has little relevance to the audience, we will find ourselves going on the trip alone. We want to avoid under-promising in the beginning of our sermons.

At the same time, we need to be careful that we do not over-promise. Our problem may even begin with the title of the sermon. Suppose in the religion section of the Saturday newspaper, this title appears for my sermon, "How to Overcome Your Problems in Marriage." Suppose I am preaching a series on practical human concerns and my title is, "How to Overcome Depression." If I am more doctrinally oriented in my preaching, the title for the sermon on Sunday morning may be, "Everything You Have Wanted to Know about the Trinity."

What will I do in the introductions to these sermons? I will either promise what I will not be able to deliver, or I will have to let them know I will not be able to say all that the title promises. Either way, disillusionment and distrust are the results. We need to be careful that in our desire to capture the attention of people, we do not make a promise for more than our sermon can keep.

Keeps Interest

When we begin a sermon, we have the attention of most people. What we must do is not get their interest but keep it. When teachers of preaching say to students that the introduction to a sermon is designed to get the attention of people, we can help create some bizarre beginnings. The pressure is on to get a big beginning, a powerful story, something that will wake everyone up. Several negative things can result.

First, the climax of the sermon may occur in the introduction, leaving the sermon to go nowhere but downhill. Emotional intensity for a congregation or for a preacher is hard to maintain throughout the sermon. If the beginning of our sermon has an overpowering story, the audience may stop listening. It is like shooting off the biggest fireworks first at the Fourth of July celebration. How do you follow that? The climax of the sermon should occur toward the end of the message. The great story or illustration may indeed get the interest of people, but the problem then becomes holding that attention.

A second problem resulting from overemphasizing introductions is in making a proper transition or connection between the beginning and body of the sermon. Transitions are important parts of a sermon. They are bridges over which we carry people from one movement to another. One breakdown in the preparation of sermons is awkward transition. This is particularly evident in the move from the introduction to the main part of the sermon and from the main part to its conclusion.

Most preachers have had the experience of hearing a gripping story. The next Sunday we begin our sermon with it whether or not it has to do with what we are trying to say. The story loses its punch. It is like trying to fit the wrong piece into the wrong place in the puzzle; it just does not work. If we make any transition from the story to our main points, it is awkward and contrived.

Over the last several years, I have become more of an advocate of beginning the sermon with the biblical text itself. This does not mean that every sermon should begin this way because we need variety in introductions. Few churches would like their pastor to begin the sermon the same way every week. It becomes too predictable.

However, I am convinced that more of our sermons should begin with the text itself. A sermon is a promise to explore a particular passage of Scripture. My covenant as a minister with the community of faith is to look at that text in the light of the struggles, decisions, demands, and needs of our lives. Whether I begin with the text or not, I need to move toward it fairly soon in the sermon. The text ought not arrive on the caboose of the train or else the preacher gives the impression, "By the way, before I am finished I had better make some mention of the text."

Part of the reason some ministers do not begin with the text is a false assumption that the Bible is boring, and that therefore we must first get the attention of the people. We believe we need to begin with something contemporary, dramatic, or humorous and then work our way back to the first century A.D.

Those who see the Bible as boring need to read a book of sermons written by an African-American minister. Long before most of us were talking about the power of retelling the biblical stories, black ministers saw the impact these stories could have on the lives of people and were telling the stories with imagination and insight. Preachers need to become a part of the text they read so that it lives, moves, and has its being in them. When that happens, the Bible is hardly boring. We will not begin a sermon with the attitude that the text is bitter medicine whose taste must be disguised.

Another reason we may resist introducing a sermon by going directly to the text is our rejection of an old form of preaching which presented the biblical material first and the application last. This style of preaching dealt with biblical matters such as historical background, explanation of certain words, and other scholarly concerns in the first part of the sermon. For those who stayed awake during the "heavy" part, the reward was, "Now, quickly, this passage says three things to our lives."

When I suggest beginning the sermon with the text, I am not promoting that approach. Preferably, weave the application throughout the biblical message so that the preacher creates a constant conversation between the Word of God and the lives of people. We want to move our listeners into the experience of the biblical text rather than merely telling them about it and the "points" it makes for their lives.

The Conclusion

Calls to Decision

One of the most complete sermons recorded in the Bible is preached by Simon Peter in Acts. Luke, the writer of Acts, says that Peter "stood up with the Eleven" and began to preach (2:14, NIV). It is an interesting picture of support.

Preaching at its best is not just *to* the church but *for* the church and *by* the church.

Luke reports the response of the people after Peter had finished preaching the sermon: "When the people heard this, they were cut to the heart and said to Peter and the other apostles, 'Brothers, what shall we do?'" (v. 37, NIV). The preaching demanded a response. The sermon was not over when the preacher had finished speaking. The nature of the proclaimed Word is that it calls for a response. "Brothers, what shall we do?" That question is a reminder that the aim of preaching is to make a difference in the lives of people. The hearers may comment about the eloquence of a particular minister; they may enjoy a sermon, remembering the effective stories or the moving style of the preacher. But what if no one who listens is called to decision? It may be classified as a good speech but not as true preaching.

When the conclusion of the sermon is seen as a call to decision, it is even more imperative that ministers be clear about what they are trying to say and do in the sermon. The conclusion should be related to the theme and the intent of the sermon. If I am preaching a sermon whose intent is to call people to accept Jesus Christ as their personal Savior, I need to focus the call to decision on that. If I am preaching in a church that issues a public invitation, I may want to mention other ways that people may respond. However, I want to make sure that I maintain the focus on evangelism. Few things hurt the impact of a sermon more than for the preacher to call people to so many things that no one feels called to anything.

Sometimes, the intent of the sermon is to teach. When speaking to a congregation confused about an issue, we may want to end the sermon by reiterating the major things we have said. In this type of sermon, the call to decision is actually a call to a clarity of thought and, through that, a call to a new commitment of life.

Another example of a sermon with a different purpose is one intended to comfort. Recently, a large, well-known church in our state lost its beautiful sanctuary to a fire. I had preached there not long before and remembered how impressed I was with the stateliness of the building. It was a magnificent place to gather to worship God.

Suppose you were the pastor of this church, and it was the Sunday after this tragedy. What would you say? You would most likely remind them that the church is people, but you would also allow them to grieve. The assurance you might give them is that while some things have died, our hope is in the Christ of the church who is still alive and at work. The call to decision on this day would be to know the comforting presence of the God who is always present, even in the midst of dramatic changes.

How we end a sermon is integrally related to what we are trying to say and do in the whole sermon. A clear conclusion and call to decision indicates a preacher who is clear in the theme and intent of the sermon.

Remains Simple

Some folks have a bias against simplicity. To them it is the opposite of profound. My own feeling is that the preacher who has done the work of preparation will be able to say the most sublime things in the simplest ways. We need to remember we are preaching to people who will hear the words one time. Some of them come to church distracted or preoccupied with their own problems and pressures. We are not presenting a term paper or a scholarly discourse. Our primary purpose is to communicate clearly.

The need for simplicity becomes even more urgent as we come to the conclusion of the sermon. Remember, what we are trying to do as preachers is to move the sermon into the lives of the listeners and have them ask, "What should I do?" We want to avoid anything that confuses or clouds this critical moment.

New ideas should not be introduced in the conclusion of the sermon. A previous idea may be restated, but it is dangerous to introduce totally new concepts in the last few minutes of the sermon. We do not have the opportunity to develop, explain, or illustrate them. If we do so, that idea usually takes over the mind of the listener and will be the thing remembered. Careful planning prevents the rushed feeling we get when the preacher says, "I'm almost finished, but before I close I want to say three important things to you." When I hear a minister say this, I want to respond, "If these things were so important, why weren't they shared through the whole sermon?"

Illustrations or stories that are lengthy or demand a heavy emotional investment from the listeners should be avoided in the conclusion. My own preference is to avoid long stories anywhere in the sermon. Stories with numerous details, twists, and turns are hard to listen to anyway. We also take a risk if we tell a long story and people do not "get it." One place where preachers are tempted to ramble is in giving unnecessary details in a story or an illustration. It is not usually necessary to tell the year it happened, whether it was winter or summer, the color of the sweater he was wearing, or who won the World Series that summer.

Some stories demand a heavy emotional investment from the hearers. They may be so powerful that people will have a hard time listening to anything else said. They will still be back on that pediatric oncology unit with that little girl and her parents who have just heard the physician say, "I'm sorry to have to tell you, but the tumor is malignant." Whenever we tell a story, we need to ask ourselves, "What impact will this have on the hearers?" I do not want to follow a story about a little girl and her parents struggling with a devastating diagnosis with an idea that will require concentrated attention from the hearers. At the conclusion of the sermon, I want the primary focus of the congregation to be on the question, "What will we do?"

One thing I often do in the conclusion is circle back to the beginning of the sermon. For example, I am preaching a sermon from John 8 entitled, "The Dawning of a New Day." The first part of chapter 8 is the story of the woman caught in adultery. In verse 2, we are given an interesting detail: "At dawn he [Jesus] appeared again in the temple courts, where all the people gathered around him, and he sat down to teach them" (NIV). John gives us the time of day: it was dawn.

I talk about the possibility of the dawning of a new day in the life of this woman because of her encounter with Jesus. At the end of the sermon, I might say something like this: "It was the dawning of the new day in the temple court in Jerusalem, and who knows, this may be the dawning of a new day for some of us."

The process of circling back to the beginning has the benefit of staying with something familiar that the congregation has already heard. Now the preacher tries to move more deeply into the experience of the hearers so that they ask, "What do we do?"

Is Brief

When Paul wrote to the Philippians, he began what is now chapter 3 with the words, "Finally, my brothers..." (v. 1, NIV). It sounded as if Paul was about to finish, but he continued for two more chapters and said again in Philippians 4:8 (NIV), "Finally, brothers...." The apostle was having difficulty in knowing how to end the letter. We have all had that experience in writing to someone who was special to us. Things keep coming to our mind, making what started out as a note to resemble a chapter in a book. It is usually acceptable in a letter. We do not expect anyone to grade a personal letter on its organization. We also have the benefit of rereading the letter and trying to understand what may have confused us the first time.

However, the same form is hardly acceptable in a sermon. Knowing how and when to end clearly and cogently is extremely important. Ministers should take time to think carefully through the conclusion to the sermon. This part of the sermon often suffers from lack of time and attention. Some of us simply run out of time before we plan the conclusion, resulting in a sermon that wanders around or dribbles off into a kind of nothingness.

Most unplanned conclusions run too long. When this happens, the temptation is to preface our closing remarks with statements like, "You may not remember anything else I have said, but I want you to remember this." It is insulting both to the preacher and to the hearers. It insinuates that people do not listen well or that the minister has said nothing memorable.

Anyone who has traveled by plane much has experienced the "holding pattern." When the air traffic is heavy, causing the controllers to handle more arriving airplanes than can land, some of the waiting planes are put in a holding pattern. The plane keeps flying around while the passengers fret about their flight connections and wonder if the plane will ever make it to the ground. There is a truth for those of us who preach. Few things are more irritating to a congregation than to be put in a holding pattern, wondering if the preacher is ever going to land this sermon. It is a great compliment if people tell their preacher they could have heard more. It is no compliment if they look at their watches during the sermon, shaking them to make sure they have not stopped.

Exercises

I. Perhaps the most difficult transition in a sermon is from the introduction to the body of sermon. Using a biblical text with which you have already worked, write an introduction that begins with the text. How quickly do you signal to the congregation that something in the sermon has a bearing on their lives?

II. Look at a book of sermons, and read closely the introduction and conclusions. Which ones catch your interest or challenge you in some way? Record the appealing aspects of the introductions and conclusions.

III. Write a conclusion that "doubles back" to the introduction and uses some of the same material. As you write the conclusion, keep in mind what you want the sermon "to do" in the lives of the listeners.

PART III

PREACHING FROM INSIDE THE GOSPEL

8

PREACHING INSIDE THE OLD TESTAMENT FROM A NEW TESTAMENT STANCE

Martin Luther said that we read the Bible forward but we understand it backwards. Christians find the fulfillment of the Old Testament, or the Hebrew Scriptures, in the coming of Jesus Christ into this world. We see the grace of God in the experiences of a prophet like Hosea, but we believe that grace is fully revealed in the face of Jesus. We see the love of God in the tender call of Jeremiah as he invited his people to a "new covenant of the heart." However, the prophet's call only foreshadows the love of God so clearly seen at Calvary. We hear about the judgment of God in the words of the Psalm, "No one from the east or the west or from the desert can exalt a man" (Ps. 75:6-7, NIV). It is in Jesus, though, that judgment finds its fulfillment as the Nazarene calls people to decide how and for eternity whether He is the "way, the truth, and the life" (John 14:6, KJV).

We may read the Bible forward, but we do understand it backwards. In Jesus the Christ we put our faith. We understand Him to be the Word that gives final meaning to all the words in the Bible.

The fact that Jesus is the fulfillment and focus of our faith means that preachers gravitate more naturally to the New Testament for their texts. This is the place where we find the life of Christ and the inspired reflection of the early church on all of His meaning for their lives. The New Testament is more familiar territory to most of us. The Old Testament contains names and places that are hard to pronounce, much less to make the center of the sermon. When I was a pastor, I found that about 75 percent of my preaching came from New Testament texts. When I did venture into the Old Testament, it was often to the very familiar passages like Psalm 23 or the story of Job.

Yet, the Old Testament is a part of our Christian canon. We speak of it as the inspired Word of God. How can we as preachers move back into the Old Testament to search its depths? How can we study these Scriptures with a sense of excitement and not just oughtness? In this chapter, we will deal with some of the resistance we have at times to preaching from the Old Testament. Then I want to look at some of the areas in which the Hebrew Scriptures can shape our perspective of life and inform our preaching.

Resistance to the Old Testament

An excellent book that focuses on preaching from the Old Testament is *Reclaiming the Old Testament for the Christian Pulpit* by Donald E. Gowan.[1] Gowan briefly discusses three reasons that we sometimes resist preaching from the Old Testament.

First, Gowan says, "The Old Testament has presented Christians with a whole series of moral problems."[2] Among the examples Gowan cites are the time that Abraham lied about his wife (Gen. 12:10-20) and the day that Elijah slaughtered the prophets of Baal at Mount Carmel (1 Kings 18:40). Many examples could be given.

In response to some of these concerns, Gowan points out that what we are often dealing with in the Bible are not perfect people but "real" people. We have wanted to use the Bible as a set of moral examples; then when we run across real people, such as Jacob or David, whose behavior was sometimes far from exemplary, we do not know what to do. If we come to the Bible looking for people who are perfect moral and spiritual examples, we will be disappointed. The Bible does not disguise the humanity of its characters.

In considering Old Testament morality, we must realize that we stand before the Bible knowing that we cannot comprehend all its meaning. We cannot wrap words around all the ways of God. Our tendency as ministers is to want to explain everything. In the process, we reduce the message of some of the Bible to our size rather than standing before a story like Abraham and Isaac, being amazed by a God who could ask so much. The result of our need to explain is that the text loses much of its power as we whittle it down to a shape and size we can manage. To read the story of Abraham and Isaac is to be confronted by a God who demands all that we are and by a man whose radical obedience led him to put everything in the hands of God. It is a message that challenges all of us; preachers who approach this text as if they have it all down pat, have reduced the size and significance of the Word.

A second difficulty Gowan mentions in dealing with the Old Testament is the cultural differences between then and now. According to Gowan, this makes some of the Old Testament seem irrelevant to us. For example, he mentions that the Old Testament people needed instructions on how to sacrifice animals. Unlike those ancient people, today we do not need to be warned against alliances with the Assyrians.

One thing Gowan warns preachers against is the "great pitfall of allegorizing."[3] It is tempting to try to relate some things in the Old Testament to the New Testament by the use of allegory. So, in Leviticus 11, the list of creatures that may not be eaten was explained by saying each creature really was a symbol of a vice Christians should avoid. And the scarlet cord, which hung from Rahab's window and saved her house from destruction (Josh. 2:18), is interpreted as the message that we are saved by the blood of Christ.[4]

The great problem with the use of allegory is that the message is not contained within the text itself and is usually built on the speculation of the preacher. That is a dangerous form of exegesis. Who controls such speculation? It may make for some interesting preaching, but it is dangerous to suggest meanings for Scripture that cannot be supported by the texts themselves.

The third reason Gowan suggests for ministers' resistance to preaching from the Old Testament is that "... much of the Old Testament seems to be untheological."[5] Take for example the Song of Songs or the Song of Solomon as it is sometimes called. How many sermons have you heard which came from this Old Testament book? Most preachers develop their own "canon within the canon." While we may affirm all of the Bible as the Word of God, most of us have our favorite parts to preach. Given a choice between the Book of Esther and the parable of the prodigal son, my decision is easy. Preachers need to expand their own personal canons in order to proclaim the whole Bible.

In addition to the three reasons Gowan gives, I would suggest two others that cause many of us to resist the Old Testament as the source for our sermons. A lack of understanding of the history of the Old Testament means that when we read certain parts of the Hebrew Scriptures, we do not understand the historical framework or context of the particular text. It is hard to drop into the middle of some part of history without understanding the events surrounding that particular episode. A good investment for any minister is a historical introduction to the Old Testament and a good Bible dictionary which gives an overview of each book and an explanation of names and places.[6]

A final reason I would suggest that makes the use of the Old Testament more difficult and challenging is the variety of literature. Some types included are history, story, hymns, proverbs, apocalyptic literature, and wisdom literature. The New Testament has a variety of literature, but not quite as much as the Old Testament. The form in which the Word comes to us needs to be taken seriously, as it does have an impact on the experience of the hearer.

Recently, I was in a worship service, and one of the Scripture texts was a psalm. Instead of reading it, the minister sang it. I was impressed that he could sing it because if I had tried that, it would have cleared the place in a hurry. More importantly, I remember the impact it had on me. The singing was deeply moving. I recalled those times when I have sat in the sanctuary and been moved by the impact of a song. Not long ago a young woman sang "Amazing Grace" at a revival service where I was preaching. We were moved that night by a song that most of us have heard many times but have never grown tired of hearing.

Gowan, in his book *Reclaiming the Old Testament for the Christian Pulpit*, suggests ways to preach from various types of literature in the Old Testament. The book by Thomas Long, *The Literary Forms of the Bible*, is also helpful. While Long does not limit his discussion to the Old Testament, he gives us a valuable understanding of the relationship of literary forms to preaching.

Lessons from the Old Testament

One of the most provocative contemporary writers in the area of preaching from the Old Testament is Elizabeth Achtemeier, adjunct professor of Bible and homiletics at Union Theological Seminary in Richmond, Virginia. In 1989, Achtemeier published an excellent book, *Preaching from the Old Testament*. In this book, she also discusses ways of preaching from the various types of literature found in the Old Testament.

Perhaps, the most controversial suggestion Achtemeier makes is that, in preaching, an Old Testament text must be paired with one from the New.[7] Achtemeier gives rationale for her position and suggests some ways the texts from the two Testaments can be brought together.

While I agree that the Christian preacher reads the Hebrew Scriptures in light of the new covenant we have in Christ, I do not believe that it is *always* necessary to have a matching New Testament text. In some instances it works well, but in others it may be a forced match. We understand as preachers that our fundamental task is to open people to the presence of God which is most fully seen in the person of Jesus. Therefore, most sermons from the Old Testament will be informed and influenced by the faith stance of the Christian preacher.

One of the most helpful chapters in the book by Elizabeth Achtemeier is entitled, "Why the Old Testament Is Necessary for the Church." She suggests four major areas in which the Old Testament is absolutely essential to our understanding. Those areas are: the nature of the world, ourselves as human beings, who God is, and who we are as the church of Jesus Christ.[8] While all of these are important, I want to emphasize two of them and add one of my own.

Who God Is

The first book of the Bible begins, "In the beginning God created the heavens and the earth" (Gen. 1:1, NIV). The existence of God is assumed, and the fact that God is alive and at work in the world is announced. Both of these facts about God are crucial as we look at the unfolding story of the Bible and the God who is the chief actor in the drama of history.

God exists! Nowhere in the Bible is there a formal argument offered for the existence of God. We do not find philosophical persuasions for those who wonder if there is a Creator behind the creation. At times, people in the Bible struggle to find the face of God or to see the shape of the providence of God, but always it is assumed there is God.

The fact that God exists means that there is purpose in life. Beyond what we see with our eyes and understand with our minds, there is a God in whom we can place our trust. Many of the Psalms capture so poignantly the tension between our own fear in the face of the difficulties of life and our faith that God is with us. Listen to the anguish of the psalmist:

> Will the Lord reject forever?
> Will he never show his favor again?
> Has his unfailing love vanished forever?
> Has his promise failed for all time?
> Has God forgotten to be merciful?
> Has he in anger withheld his compassion?
> (Ps. 77:7-9, NIV)

Then the psalmist begins to remember the ways that God has rescued His people in the past. Remembering became the writer's reassurance for the future, and he closed the psalm with these words of faith:

> Your path led through the sea,
> your way through the mighty waters,
> though your footprints were not seen.
> You led your people like a flock
> by the hand of Moses and Aaron.
>
> (Ps. 77:19-20, NIV)

This theme of despair and hope reminds us of the Good Friday/Easter message that is at the heart of our faith as Christians. On Friday at Calvary, God seemed absent. Even Jesus cried, "My God, my God, why hast thou forsaken me?" (Mark 15:34, KJV). Despair filled the air as a few of the disciples stood at the foot of the cross, but most of them had scattered trying to make some sense of life without the young Galilean.

Friday is followed by the silence of Saturday. To the disciples it seemed as if God was dead; what can be said when the purpose and power for life are wrenched from us? But Sunday is only a day away, and with the dawning of the sun comes the dawning of a new Hope. The message that Jesus is alive means once again that He is present to His people and to the world.

"In the beginning God," the author of Genesis wrote. He affirmed the existence of God who was alive even before creation. However, that is not all the writer said, "In the beginning God *created*." The picture painted was of a God alive and actively at work in the world.

To believe in the existence of a God is one thing, but it is quite another to believe God cares enough to involve and invest Himself in the life of His creation. This is the God of the Old Testament. God takes initiative. He beckons, calls, directs, undergirds, sustains, and strengthens. God wants to be in relationship with creation. God wants to bless the world through His people, Israel. The God of the Old Testament is a God who wants to save even the Ninevites, liberate the oppressed, give power to the powerless, and, through the prophets, calls people to justice, mercy, and humility.

As preachers we deprive our hearers if we do not preach this kind of God whose hand is on the history of our lives. We want people to know that from the outset of biblical history, God has been alive and at work in our world. We want to preach that even in our sin God has not given up on us. More than anything else, God wants us to be in relationship with Him. God is constantly seeking to get back that which belongs to Him.

Who We Are

If God wants to be in relationship to us, what does this say about us? Are human beings simply a biological accident? Did we evolve to what we are apart from any plan or purpose of God? Or is there something very special about us as a part of the creation of God?

The Book of Genesis says that we are created in the image of God. Biblical scholars debate all the ramifications, but we know that there is something special about being created in His image. While pride continues to be a problem in our time, another problem is that many people think too little of themselves.

Think about your Sunday morning congregation. How many see themselves as unique creations of God, loved by God, sought by God, and known by God? Many of us still struggle with the issue of self-worth. We nod our heads at the message of the grace of God, but our hearts resist it. To all of us still struggling to receive the message of our acceptance by God, the Old Testament presents us with a God who does the most amazing things with the most unlikely people.

That concept is a strong part of the message of who we are. God does not look for perfection when He selects His servants. Abraham, Sarah, Moses, David, Jeremiah—all these and many more are presented with their failures and foibles. What we see in the Old Testament is not the achievements of perfect people. Rather, we see what God can do in a life that yields itself to Him.

The Old Testament not only stresses the relationship of God to humankind but also emphasizes the relationship of people to each other and to the world to which God has called them to be stewards. In the creation story, God saw the man alone and said, "'It is not good for the man to be alone. I will make a helper suitable for him'" (Gen. 2:18, NIV). While this text is most often used at wedding ceremonies, it is more than an endorsement of marriage. It is a call to community and to see our need for each other.

Community is constantly broken by the results of our sin, and the Bible hardly begins before a brother kills a brother. Warfare, bitterness, envy, murder—these are all part of the landscape of the Hebrew Scriptures. Israel was called to be a blessing to other nations, but Israel had to be reminded again and again that God's call to them was to get *and* to give. Jonah preached to the Ninevites, but he despised them. People hurt or ignored each other, but the vision of God for creation was expressed in the moving words of Isaiah:

> The wolf will live with the lamb,
> the leopard will lie down with the goat,
> the calf and the lion and the yearling together;
> and a little child will lead them.
> The cow will feed with the bear,
> their young will lie down together,
> and the lion will eat straw like the ox.
> The infant will play near the hole of the cobra,
> and the young child put his hand into the viper's
>   nest.
> They will neither harm nor destroy
>   on all my holy mountain,
> for the earth will be full of the knowledge of the Lord
> as the waters cover the sea.
>   (Isa. 11:6-9, NIV)

The Old Testament calls us to be responsible to each other, and it also calls us to responsibility for all of creation.

The pronouncement after each part of creation was, "God saw that it was good" (Gen. 1:10,12,18,21,25, NIV). After He created Adam, "God saw all that he had made, and it was very good" (1:31, NIV). God called the creature made in God's image to be a steward or manager of all that was so good (1:28).

We are reaping the consequences today of the abuse of creation. Some of us who are Christians have allowed others to speak out on environmental concerns while we have remained silent. As preachers, we have an opportunity and obligation to speak about a theology of the stewardship of all of God's gifts. We are called to remind people that this is God's world, and the word of the Creator is, "It is good."

Adversity and Suffering

Several years ago a Jewish Rabbi, Harold Kushner, wrote the book *When Bad Things Happen to Good People*. I did not agree with all of his conclusions, but I was grateful for the sensitivity of Rabbi Kushner to the subject and for the tremendous interest people had in the matter of suffering. Kushner touched a nerve, and the book became a runaway bestseller.

People are concerned about adversity and suffering. Preachers speak of the goodness of God, and yet we live in a world of natural and personal disasters. We all look for explanations and strength to deal with those difficult times in our lives.

If someone is drunk, runs into a telephone pole, and kills himself, we may say that person has reaped the consequences of his behavior. However, if that same man runs into a bus carrying a church youth group, killing or injuring many of the young people, how do we explain that to the parents called to the hospital?

Much contemporary preaching seems to emphasize that "right" living will produce prosperity, pleasure, and material abundance. Several prominent television preachers base their appeal on the fact that God does not want us to suffer or be sick. These preachers build their theology on such verses as Proverbs 11:8 (NIV), "The righteous man is rescued from trouble, and it comes on the wicked instead." The impression given to people is that if they are not well and prosperous, they have a problem with their faith.

The difficulty with this theology is that it contains some half-truths. Faithfulness to God has its rewards; although those blessings are not always material, as some would have us believe. In fact, the deepest blessings of life cannot be bought at the counter of a department store. Peace of mind cannot be purchased for any amount of money. The false promise that if we do certain things in life, certain results will always happen creates great disillusionment in the minds of people. This reduces life to an exact equation that is not always absolute.

Of all the Old Testament books dealing with the issue of suffering, none is more graphic than the story of Job. It centers around a fundamental question, "Why do the righteous suffer?"

In the end Job was rewarded with all that was taken away from him, plus more. We recognize that does not always happen in the lives of godly people. Some people go to their grave with the void still in their lives, but as Christian ministers, we preach the hope of heaven.

I had just graduated from college when I performed my first funeral. A young couple had lost their baby. I stood with them and a few of their family and friends, speaking about the presence of God in our pain and the hope that we have because of the resurrection of Christ from the dead. I walked away from the cemetery that day knowing that a part of my ministry was going to be calling people to try to see the "hope of glory."

As painful as suffering is, it can be a great teacher for our lives. The preacher who wants to eliminate all pain assumes that pain in itself is always wrong. On the contrary, some who have spoken most profoundly to my life have had seasons of suffering in which they have come to know the sufficiency of God.

In the time of Job's questioning, God spoke to him with questions of His own. Chapter 38 is a series of questions from God to Job designed to let Job know that he has been created to depend on God. We are not always promised deliverance from our pain, but we are promised the strength of God if we depend upon Him.

As I have mentioned, in the days following the illness of our son, I preached a series of sermons from Psalm 23. I am certain that I selected this shepherd's song as much for myself as for the congregation. One week while preparing a sermon on verse four, I was struck in a new way by the promise of the first part of that verse: "Yea though I walk through the valley of the shadow of death, I will fear no evil, for Thou art with me" (KJV).

Those last five words became bread for my journey. The psalmist said there will be valleys and dark stretches. He did not profess to understand all of the dimensions of the darkness. What undergirded the shepherd was the presence of Another who guides and guards. That is our assurance: "For Thou art with me."

Ken Hemphill in the conclusion to *Reclaiming the Prophetic Mantle* speaks to the New Testament use of the Old Testament this way:

> The Christian church was born on the day of Pentecost with sacred Scriptures: the Law, the Prophets, and the Writings. The earliest Christians were Jews, and the Scriptures were the literary foundation of their confession of faith in the crucified and risen Messiah, Jesus. The distinctive difference between the Jews who became Christians and those who rejected the messianic claims being made about Jesus centered around the proper reading of the Scriptures. The non-Christian Jews saw no expectation of a crucified Messiah, whereas the Christians declared that the ancient Scriptures did predict such a Messiah. Thus, the Christian reading of Scripture would often differ dramatically from the interpretive traditions of their Jewish heritage, but they were convinced

that their new readings were coherent and consistent with the divine purposes accomplished in the history of Israel as revealed in the sacred texts.[9]

The Christian preacher must get inside the living text of the Old Testament. In so doing the preacher will find the "Old" Word and the "New" Word are part of God's Word. The criteria for understanding and preaching this Word is Jesus Christ, God incarnate.

Exercises

I. How often do you preach from the Old Testament? If you have difficulty doing so, make your own list of reasons why you resist preaching from the Old Testament.

II. Select several psalms at random, and read them out loud. Write down what they say to you about God, yourself, adversity, suffering, or anything else that captures your imagination.

Notes

1. Donald E. Gowan, *Reclaiming the Old Testament for the Christian Pulpit* (Edinburgh: T & T Clark Ltd., 1980), 3.

2. Ibid.

3. Ibid., 4.

4. Ibid.

5. Ibid., 6.

6. For example, *Holman Bible Dictionary* (Nashville: Holman Bible Publishers, 1991 and Paul House, *Old Testament Survey* (Nashville: Broadman Press, 1992) or Robert L. Cate, *An Introduction to the Old Testament and Its Study* (Nashville: Broadman Press, 1987).

7. Elizabeth Achtemeier, *Preaching From the Old Testament* (Louisville, Ky.: Westminster/John Knox Press, 1989), 56-59.

8. Ibid., 21-26.

9. George L. Klein, *Reclaiming the Prophetic Mantle* (Nashville: Broadman Press, 1992).

⌐9⌐

STYLES AND STORIES
THAT GET THE GOSPEL OUT

We have all been affected by preachers who have shaped
the kind of preacher we have become. As I look back at my
own life, I would name three ministers who have been
formative in my own development.

The first is Billy Graham. I have admired the passion and
energy this great evangelist has brought to his ministry. He
seems to believe what he says, and I have been grateful for
his strength of conviction and the power of his delivery.

The second preacher who influenced me greatly is John
Claypool. John was pastor of the Crescent Hill Baptist
Church when I was a student at Southern Baptist Theological Seminary in Louisville, Kentucky. John Claypool
brought a depth to preaching that impressed me. For the
first time in my life, I saw demonstrated in this pastor the
power of confessional preaching. While some may criticize
John for overusing personal illustrations in the sermon, few
who were in Louisville at the time will ever forget the
moving messages he brought during the illness and death
of his daughter, Laura Lue. Published later as *Tracks of a
Fellow Struggler*,[1] these sermons have helped multitudes of
people through the valley of the shadow of death.

Fred Craddock is the third preacher who has had a significant impact on my perception of preaching. Through his
books, conferences with him, and the opportunity to spend a
four month sabbatical with him at Candler Theological
Seminary, Fred Craddock has taught me about the adven-

ture of entering a biblical text to seek a message and the excitement of shaping that message into a sermon.

Others have helped me. My own colleagues in the department of preaching at Southern Seminary have taught me many things. Raymond Bailey, James Cox, and Craig Loscalzo have assisted me immensely both in the way they preach and in their teaching of homiletics.

In recalling those who have influenced me, I am struck by two things. First, I am grateful to these people and to others for what they have meant to me. The second thing that impresses me is the diversity of a group like Billy Graham, John Claypool, and Fred Craddock. I am talking about more than theological diversity. These men have distinctly different styles of preaching.

It serves as a reminder to us that there is no such thing as a "single, successful sermon style." Think about the preachers that have had an impact on your own style, and I dare say that you will be struck by their differences as well as their similarities. It is amazing that God is able to use so many different types of personalities and different kinds of gifts to communicate the wonders of His Word.

While acknowledging that there is no one style for all preachers to be good communicators, I want to discuss four characteristics that mark most preachers who are effective in what they do.

Conviction

When we stand to preach, do we believe that God can use what we say to change the lives of people? Do we have the deep conviction that preaching can make a difference because we know the Christ whom we proclaim can make a difference in the lives of those who listen as well as in our own?

Each semester I teach a class at the seminary entitled "preaching *practicum*." The students preach in the class and receive feedback from their fellow students and from me. I begin the semester by telling the students that we all can do things to be better communicators of the gospel. This certainly includes their professor. I hardly ever preach a sermon when I do not reflect on how it could have been better. Becoming a more effective preacher is a lifelong pursuit because our goal is to present evermore clearly and winsomely the God who has come to us in Jesus Christ.

Many mistakes preachers make can and will be forgiven by their congregations. Yet, the one unforgivable sin of preaching is to speak as if what is said makes no difference. I can listen to different kinds of preaching, but my anger is drawn by hearing someone speak about the ultimate things of life in a matter of fact, "so what" kind of way.

I will never forget the day a certain young man was preaching in one of my classes. It was obvious he was afraid. He did not have the experience some others in the class had in preaching. The words did not flow as they had for others. No one would have used the words "eloquent" or "articulate" to describe him. However, as he preached, I noticed the class and I were listening to every word. It had become more than a preaching class. It was a time of worship, and we were listening for the Word of God to our lives.

The difference was that he was speaking about the Christ whom he deeply loved. Something had changed his life, and he wanted us to know about it. The text he was preaching from had meaning for him. He had not merely read the words; he had lived with them, encompassed them in his life, and truly wanted them to be a part of our lives. This student was not as concerned about impressing us with his preaching ability as he was impressing upon us the One who had changed his life. We knew that for the moments of his sermon we were on holy ground because we were listening to someone who was preaching from the inside out.

There is no sure-fire method to teach conviction, but it is something every teacher of preaching must emphasize. We are teaching more than a craft. We are trying to help students be the most effective communicators of the most important message in the world. We must continually remind them and ourselves that the "who" and "what" of our preaching can make a difference in the lives of each of us.

Clarity

In putting together a sermon, it is important to keep in mind how the message is heard by the listener. Hopefully, the preacher will go through the sermon a number of times before speaking, but the congregation has only one opportunity to hear it. As preachers, we pray over our words, study the message, visualize the sermon, listen to the impact for our lives; but those who listen only have one chance to hear the words and grasp the meaning.

We need to remember that sermon preparation is not like writing a term paper in college. Technical terms and complex reasoning may have been appropriate to impress our professor, but for most congregations they are confusing rather than enlightening. This is not to insult the intelligence of the people who are listening. Instead, we should recognize that most of us listen better to phrases that are concise, to vocabulary that is simple, and to ideas that are given images so that we can see them as well as hear them.

Ministers who insist on using theologically technical language are often perceived as pedantic and even as arrogant. Most of those who hear us are aware that we have attended seminary or received some training for our ministry; it is not necessary to show our credentials every Sunday. Our task is to speak in ways that people will hear so that they will leave knowing more of God who goes with them into their corner of the world.

With regard to clarity, I want to reemphasize the importance of knowing clearly what we want to say in the sermon. Many student sermons I hear contain too much material to develop in one sermon. Young ministers often fear that they will not have enough to say, so they take the trip from the first Adam to the final Apocalypse. The resulting sermon is rushed and overloads the minds of the listeners with too much information. When we say "yes" to the theme of our sermon, we have to say "no" or "later in another sermon" to other things. Blessed is the preacher who has learned to say "no" and "later."

Contrast

Between Story and Explanation

The last 25 years have witnessed a new emphasis on story or narrative. This is true in areas other than homiletics. Much of the theology that is being written today stresses the power of narrative.

In the area of preaching, those who have written about stories have reminded us of several vital things. Writers and preachers such as Edmund Steimle, Eugene Lowry, and others have reacquainted us with the potency of stories. Stories are not just decorations for the sermon or windows to let the congregation get some air before we get back to the real sermon. Rather, stories stand on their own and effect changes of their own in our lives.

Consider the preaching of Jesus. The fifteenth chapter of Luke is really a response to the question, "What is God like?" How did Jesus respond? Not with a learned treatise about God or a term paper with footnotes, but Jesus answered that question with three stories. God is like a shepherd who goes after the lost sheep; God is like a woman who will not rest until she has found her lost coin; and God is like a father who desperately wants both of his sons to come home.

Some have called this use of stories the recovery of the "Jewishness" of our preaching. The Greeks were highly analytical, deductive, and logical in their speaking. They have shaped our preaching through the centuries. The Jews were more oriented to story and to images, as reflected in Jesus' use of things around Him to illustrate the most profound matters of the kingdom of God.

I want to join those who celebrate this rediscovery of the power of story, images, and illustrations in preaching. At the same time, I do not believe that a diet of strictly narrative preaching is satisfying for most congregations. They want to hear some words of explanation or interpretation from their preacher. They deserve more than just a story or a succession of stories; they need to hear a clear word about life, God, faith, hope, and the need for love.

What appears to be emerging in these days is a balance between explanation and story. The pendulum is swinging back toward the middle. This may produce the kind of preaching that has interest and, at the same time, clearly presents the call and claim of Christ on all of our lives.

Between Heart and Head

I remember when I met my future wife and experienced falling in love. I recall partially making that decision with my head. Diane had those qualities I had been looking for in someone. We seemed to share common values and a similar vision for what we wanted in life. At the same time, however, this experience involved my heart. I lost my appetite (which I have since regained) and had a hard time thinking about anything else but her. I found myself sitting in class with my mind wandering to the next time we would be together.

Most of the important commitments we make in life are made with our head and our heart. At a time in my life when I was struggling with the will of God, I asked a university president how he made his most important decisions. He said that he gathered all the facts in the situation and then followed what his heart told him to do.

In preaching we need to remember that people have both minds and emotions. Both need to be considered in the way we construct and deliver the sermon. The best sermon is the one with an appeal to both the head and the heart.

There is no excuse for preaching that requires people to leave their head outside the church. In the Great Commandment, Jesus taught His disciples to love God with all of their mind, heart, and soul. Some preachers make their living by attacking education or by riding the horse of anti-intellectualism. The result is a kind of demagoguery that creates unwarranted suspicion toward education. Ministers need to use the minds God has given them and to love God with all of that mind. Likewise, they need to call their listeners to love God with all of their minds.

At the same time, we need to remember that people, including ourselves, not only "think" about life but also "feel" it. People are not changed merely by being given new ideas. I know far more about the Christian faith than I live. I listen to the apostle Paul talk again and again about being "in Christ." I am still trying to understand and to appropriate the power and peace that being "in Christ" can bring to my life. What changes us is a motivation and a new strength for living. That is a message for both head and heart.

Between Laughter and Seriousness

Some years ago a church member gave me a porcelain figure of a minister. I keep it on a shelf in my office partially as a reminder of what I do not want to be. He looks so serious. In fact, he looks as if he has fallen out of love with life and as if he has the weight of the world on his shoulders.

I realize that the work of the ministry is important. In fact, few things irritate me as much as a lazy minister. People in any kind of ministry know it is a demanding call; if we take it seriously, it requires much from us.

Although preaching is demanding, we need to remember that it is actually God's ministry. The grace of God sustains us and strengthens us all the day long. One of the vocational hazards of ministry is depression and burnout. I have found that my own periods of depression are related to those times when I feel that I bear the weight of the work. When I begin to preach as if the kingdom of God were riding on my performance, I immediately set myself up for despair. I begin to take myself too seriously and not to take God seriously enough. The result is that laughter and joy get squeezed out of my life.

I want to be intense in my preaching. I want to approach my calling with passion. But I also need to balance those desires with the humility that recognizes that I depend upon God and that God does not depend on me. God's grace frees me to see both the tears and the laughter in the Bible and then to proclaim the Bible's "good news."

Another matter to consider is the use of humor in preaching. Where do we find funny stories? Humor is found in the Bible itself if we read it with our imaginations wide open. There is also humor in life all around us.

Recently, my daughter was married. For the first part of the ceremony, I was in the traditional role of the father. I gave her away, and then I performed the rest of the wedding ceremony. When the minister who was assisting me asked, "Who gives this woman to be married to this man?" it dawned on me that these may be the silliest words we ever say in church. As the father of the bride, I can assure you there was no "giving." I paid lots of money to become the number two man in the life of my daughter. No wonder fathers of the bride have such a pained expression as they walk their daughters to the front of the church.

When I think about my experience, I am reminded how close laughter and tears are. For a week after the wedding, I walked around in a daze. It still brings tears to my eyes to think about how quickly the little girl we were sending off to kindergarten grew up and got married.

The experiences of life, everything that happens around us and to us, afford a rich storehouse of stories and illustrations. I always carry with me a small notebook in which I record things that happen and my reactions to them. The everyday patterns of our lives are rich with experiences. Happy is the congregation whose pastor preaches in a way that reflects attention to life.

I want to issue three warnings about the use of humor. First, be careful that the humor is not offensive to some people. Ethnic jokes, stories that make fun of people, and humor simply designed to draw attention to itself should be avoided. Second, preachers are not called to be stand-up comedians. When I hear a minister treat preaching as if it were an after dinner speech where the objective is to make people laugh and feel good, I wonder if that preacher understands the goal of a sermon. Our aim is to make Jesus

Christ known. Finally, while I sometimes use a standard joke, I usually try to find humor either in some life situation or in the text. The problem with using jokes is that most of the good ones have been told repeatedly. I never begin a sermon with a joke because what may have seemed funny to me in the study may die a painful death in the sanctuary. Those who have begun sermons with jokes that received no laughter or only a few polite snickers know that it is like digging a hole. We spend the rest of the sermon trying to climb out of it.

Between Words and Pause

When we think of preaching, we usually think of words. We can remember ministers who impressed us with their use of words. They used words that moved people; they crafted the words into phrases that stayed planted in our minds; they were eloquent, but not in the sense of trying to draw attention to themselves. Rather they used their words to point people to the eternal Word of God.

John said, "The Word became flesh" (John 1:14, NIV), and every Sunday a preacher stands to try to flesh out that gift of God in words that point beyond themselves. The primary tool of our trade as preachers is words. Every minister should be a student of words because they are the vehicle that God has chosen to carry the message.

While words are vitally important, the creative use of pauses can be effective in preaching. So many times we are concerned about the flow of the words in our sermon that we forget the power of a pause. This is not a pause filled with "uh's and aah's" as we desperately search for the next word. Rather, it is the kind of pause that comes as we stand in front of the sermon and feel its impact on our own lives.

Using pauses effectively is one reason that we need to "feel" the sermon as well as learn the sequence of ideas or words. I encourage the students in preaching classes to make the "experience" of the text a part of the preparation. Then when they preach, they can feel what they are saying. The tendency of students is to write out their sermons and memorize the sequence of words. The test of preparation then becomes how many words they can remember in their proper order without looking at their notes.

However, getting the words right does not mean that either the preacher or the hearers will get the message. Sometimes we stand before such powerful mysteries or potentially life-changing truths that there needs to be a sense of awe and wonder. Our pace of delivery needs to reflect that. We need to avoid the impression that we can easily wrap words around all the ways and wonders of God. When I preach about the cross of Christ, I am overwhelmed by the love that God has for me. Sometimes, I just need to bring the hearers to the foot of the cross and let them stand there and look for a moment.

The most important things in life are the hardest to put into words. When I was on sabbatical, I was away from my wife and family for several weeks at a time. When I talked with Diane on the phone, I wanted to tell her that I loved her. Suppose I had said, "Diane, I have been thinking about my love for you and I want to share five reasons for my love." That is too slick, too detached. Just "I love you" will do, and if you listen carefully, there is a catch in my throat.

With regard to the telling of stories or illustrations in the sermon, pauses are particularly effective. I tell students to remind them as well as myself, "Do not rush the story and do not preach it." Be economical with the use of words. Do not say too much. As you tell the story, experience it again yourself so that you are describing it from the inside out. Do not write out a story and then read it. Visualize the story and tell us about the picture you are seeing and experiencing. When you are finished with the story, give the congregation a moment to absorb it. Do not rush out of the illustration with some comment like, "Now let me tell you what this means or what this says to us...."

Confession/Self-Disclosure

This is an area where preachers and teachers of preaching have strong differences of opinion. As I have mentioned,

I was deeply affected by the preaching of John Claypool for whom confession is a pivotal model. I may not agree with John Claypool on certain things that should or should not be shared and perhaps on his overuse at times of the confessional model, but I heard in his preaching an authenticity and openness that drew me not just to him but to the Holy One whom he revealed in his preaching.

At the other extreme are those ministers who avoid any references to themselves. The legitimate concern of many of them is that the focus may be taken off of Christ and put on the minister. Revelations about the preacher rather than the revelation of God in Jesus Christ may become the center of preaching.

This tendency is a danger of confessional preaching. As ministers we should never give the impression that God works only within the boundaries of our limited experiences. Confessional preaching must resist the temptation of being self-serving. Our goal in preaching is not to have people glorify us or feel pity for us. Our goal is to present the reality of Jesus Christ, and every story of any kind that we use needs to contribute to the service of that truth.

Some of the benefits and pitfalls of self-disclosure were discussed in Chapter Six, so I will not repeat them. However, I want to close this look at confessional preaching by saying that my affirmation of it flows out of my own view of preaching. When we come to a biblical text to seek a message, we bring with us a picture of our listeners. We know some of their stories, their hopes, their fears, and the "shared story" that we all need something beyond ourselves. Specifically, we need to know God who has made Himself known through Jesus Christ. As preachers we need to ask, "What do people need to hear for their lives?"

We also bring ourselves, as well as our congregations, to the Word of God. We are also listening because we, too, are people with hopes, fears, and a story. We do not come to the Bible just to find a word for others. We come because we need to hear the Word for our own lives. It is legitimate for the preacher to ask, "What is God saying to me?"

If the process of preparation ends with that question, then preaching becomes selfish and self-centered. Preachers are not called to bind up their wounds every Sunday or to assume that everyone needs what they need. However, if we listen for the Word of God and allow it to confront our lives, then when we preach, we can speak out of something happening to us and through us. This is passion for preaching—when preachers speak about that which makes the difference to themselves and to all who have ears to hear.

Exercises

I. Think of several preachers who have influenced your approach to preaching. What similarities do they share? What differences do they have? If someone were to select you as a model for preaching, what would you like that person to mention as being most influential about your preaching?

II. Think of someone in your city or town who is admired by many as an effective preacher. Listen to or watch a tape of that person. What is the style of preaching like? Does it stay close to the biblical text? Is the message clear? Does the sermon relate to life? Is there any humor? What other features about the sermon would you note as effective in communicating the message?

Note

1. John Claypool, *Tracks of a Fellow Struggler: How to Handle Grief* (Waco: Word Books, 1974).

┌ 10 ┐

PREACHING THE GOSPEL INSIDE OUT: DELIVERING THE SERMON

Preaching is hard work and requires discipline on the part of the minister. I will usually say something like this early in the introductory course in preaching at the seminary because I have found that some students have come looking for a magic potion to make preaching easy and successful. Somewhere, they have in their minds, someone has a shortcut to successful sermons. "How to be a Great Preacher in Three Easy Lectures" would be a title that would draw some ministers eager to know how to "shine" on Sunday and "recline" the rest of the week.

Some ministers have a facility for preaching and seem to do well without a lot of discipline and preparation. However, I am convinced that if preaching is to be meaningful to us and to our hearers over a period of time, it demands our best. We need to have something to say, and we need to say it as clearly and powerfully as we can.

In this final chapter, I want to examine the delivery of the sermon. Some ministers thrive on the work of the study. They enjoy the encounter with the biblical text. They relish the hours they spend searching through the commentaries. They even like the process of putting the sermon into a form to be preached. However, when they move from the study to the sanctuary, from developing the sermon to delivering the sermon, it is not heard by the people in the pews. Many of them appreciate the work of their pastor. They can tell that

Preaching the Gospel Inside Out
the preacher has taken time to prepare, but the message does not seem to be heard.

Preachers are called to take seriously both the development and the delivery of the sermon. We are persons of the study and of the sanctuary. We need to know how to be alone and how to be with others in preaching. So let's move to the sanctuary and ask the question, "How then do we preach?"

Before We Preach

How we deliver the sermon begins before the chiming of the hour or the call to worship. We can do some things that will help bring us to the moment of preaching with a sense of anticipation and excitement. I have divided this pre-sermon preparation into three parts.

Spiritual Preparation

The danger for those who preach on a regular basis is that preaching can simply become a part of the routine of ministry. We go through the motions and speak the words. We may even manufacture some sense of excitement, but the truth is that every Sunday morning is just another Sunday morning. Preaching becomes dry as dust, and while we embrace the Eternal with our words, we speak with ashes in our mouth.

Most of us have had moments in our ministry like this, and we know the pain of it. The people to whom we speak assume that we know the God about whom we talk. They take for granted that we live on intimate terms with the Divine. Little do they know the enormous energy it takes at times for us to come to the pulpit and preach to them about a God who seems distant from us. No wonder so many preachers burn out. Where does the minister go to become reacquainted with God? With all of the pressures "to do" in the ministry, where do we find the time "to be" with God? It is hard to keep saying something when there seems so little time to listen for something to say.

I have no easy answers. I wish I did. I wish that I had had

them for myself in those moments when as a pastor I felt as if I were drowning in a sea of demands, and I desperately longed for a "Sabbath" where I could be still and know God. I had to recognize that much of the impulse for conducting my life this way was inside me. While most churches expect a great deal from their minister, much of the demand was coming from my own need to be wanted, to be needed, to be the perfect pastor and preacher. I was compulsively busy because I had decided that the road of achievement would take me to the destination of acceptance by others and acceptance by my own self. Somewhere in my mind existed the one thing (I did not know what it was and still do not) I could do that would make me feel that I had finally arrived. The result was that I experienced those "dark nights of the soul" in which I continued saying something even though I had taken little time with God to have anything to say.

The illness of our son David was the painful catalyst that caused me to rethink some basic things about my life. His illness was diagnosed just two and a half months after I became pastor of the First Baptist Church in Augusta, Georgia. First Baptist carries the prestige of being the "mother church" of the Southern Baptist Convention. It is a large congregation filled with some of the finest folks I know. Ministerially speaking, I had arrived.

Yet, as I sat in the pastor's study one day shortly after learning about David's illness, I was struck by the way I had misplaced my priorities. In that painful time in my own life, I saw that I had invested the best of myself in trying to become something in the eyes of others; now, I would trade it all for the health of one little boy.

At times, I have students in class who believe that they have been sent to the kingdom for such a time as this. A few of them wonder how the kingdom has managed to survive without their presence. I like their enthusiasm. As a professor, I would much rather bank a fire than build a fire. Nevertheless, it becomes important for me to remind them in their zeal and ambition, that the goal is not to build a personal kingdom. The goal is to be servant ministers who listen not only to the needs of the church but also to the needs of their families and to their own needs as well. I share these things because they are important to me and because the temptation is there to give ourselves to the ministry and the work rather than giving ourselves to the God who calls us first to Himself and then to His task.

There are two things I try to do before entering the pulpit to help me be spiritually prepared. First, I remind myself of the significance of the sermon. Going into the pulpit, I want to have fresh in my mind not just what I am going to say (the sense of the sermon) but also the "why" or the "so what" of this message (the significance of the sermon). I want to walk into the pulpit believing that God may say something through the sermon of ultimate and eternal significance. That gives intensity and passion to the preacher.

Second, I want to remember that God chooses to work through the foolishness of preaching to speak to the lives of people. This relieves me of the burden of believing that I have to make the difference with my words. My words are the means, not the end. The final prayer of preachers before entering the pulpit should be, "Whatever happens now, it is in your hands, God, and I am in your hands."

Mental Preparation

On particularly busy weeks as a pastor, I had a fantasy. The church would own a beautiful condominium either in the mountains or at the beach. I would live there during the week, return to the church to deliver the sermons, and then leave immediately. No one in the church would be allowed to tell me about any problems, and I would never have to attend another meeting. I would just be the preacher.

As far as I know, that is pure fantasy. Maybe some preacher has such an arrangement, but the ministers I know are preachers, pastors, counselors, administrators, and a host of other things. I am not sure that my fantasy would have been good even if I had found some church to accept it. I am still convinced that the best preaching is done by a minister who faithfully listens to and lives in the lives of people. "I sat where they sat," Ezekiel said (3:15, KJV). When he stood to speak, he knew what the people were experiencing.

The challenge is to learn to concentrate on the sermon in the midst of the busyness. As a pastor, I devoted most of my mornings to study and sermon preparation. I let the congregation know that I saw preaching as my most important pastoral task and that I needed concentrated periods of time to be alone. The people in the church knew I could be interrupted for an emergency and would return their phone calls if it was not an emergency.

On the day before I was to preach, I would take several hours in the morning and about an hour on Saturday evening to go through the sermon. I would visualize how I would preach it and what response I was hoping the people would have. I did not write a manuscript, but I had an outline. I would think and talk through the outline constantly asking myself, "What am I wanting to say and what difference do I want this sermon to make in the lives of the listeners?" I paid special attention to transitions to make sure I knew how I wanted to move through the sermon. As I went through the sermon, I paid close attention to the emotional content of words and phrases. I can usually tell when preaching students have spent all their time learning the order of the words but have not felt the impact of the words. Everything sounds the same. "Isn't it a nice day" is said in the same tone of voice as "Zacchaeus, I want to go home with you." The emotive power of the words is lost.

However we choose to prepare, we need some time after the words, the outline, or the structure of the sermon is fashioned to move back through the message and allow it to become alive in us. Then, when we stand on Sunday, we preach a sermon that we know, not just know about.

Physical Preparation

Several months ago I went out early to run on the Emory University track. I was doing my usual slow pace when I saw ten of the most athletic people I had ever seen. I had no idea who they were. I asked someone and found out that they were the finalists to represent the United States in the decathlon in the 1992 Summer Olympics. Talk about personal intimidation. These athletes, who have to participate in ten difficult track and field events, are among the most conditioned athletes in the world. I stayed on the track a few more minutes before my ego had all it could take. It will surprise no one that none of the people watching that day confused me for a candidate for the Olympic team.

I share that experience to say that when I talk about physical preparation for the ministry, I do not mean that we have to look and perform like an athlete. If that were the case, some of us would be eliminated from the ministry immediately. However, I am talking about taking care of the body that God has given to us.

Preaching is physically demanding. Follow most preachers home on Sunday afternoon, and you will find a tired minister. In the time of Jesus, the teacher usually sat down while the listeners stood. In John 8:2 (NIV) we are told, "He [Jesus] appeared again in the temple courts, where all the people gathered around him, and he sat down to teach them." Try that the next time you preach, and you will have rebellion on your hands. Some people in our churches get edgy when they have to stand on all of the stanzas of a hymn.

Preachers have to make the decision to take care of themselves. Some people go into the ministry expecting other people to take care of them or to set their boundaries and limits. While most people in a church genuinely care about their minister, they will usually take all that person is willing to give. We need to follow the example of Jesus who found it necessary at times to renew Himself by moving away from the demands. If we never have time for ourselves using the excuse that we have too much to do, we may need to ask where our demands originate. Do they all come from outside of us, or is there inside of us the compulsive need to be liked, to say yes, or to be all things to all people so that we might somehow win the approval of others and our-selves?

When We Preach

Much of the way that we deliver a sermon is affected by the way we prepare ourselves spiritually, mentally, and physically. At this point, I want to talk about some matters that relate to the delivery of the sermon itself.

The Voice of Preaching: How Do I Speak?

When we talk about the delivery of a sermon, it seems as if we have entered the realm of the practical. We may think that theology affects such things as the hermeneutics of preaching, but it certainly has nothing to do with delivery.

On the contrary, claiming our own voice for preaching may say more to us about our acceptance of the grace of God than most anything else. As I have said, most of us have been affected by preachers who have modeled effective proc-lamation. That is one of the ways most of us learn about preaching. I frequently watch videotapes of ministers I ad-mire and observe the way they structure sermons, tell sto-ries, use words and phrases, make transitions, and begin and end sermons.

The problem arises when we become so overwhelmed by a particular model that we begin to imitate that preacher. Our voice becomes that preacher's voice. The theological issue is the refusal to accept the gift that God has given to us. It is a denial of our own gift of grace.

Some preachers have adopted the "stained-glass voice syndrome" in the pulpit. They preach as if there is a proper way every preacher should sound. In our desire to be "every preacher," we sacrifice the uniqueness that God has given to us.

There is a difference between our public and private selves as preachers. I will sound somewhat different in a sanctuary speaking to a thousand people than in my study talking to one person. The problem comes when my public self is so different that those who know me best wonder if I am still the same husband and father who lives in their house. "Was that really you up there tonight, Dad?" is not a compliment.

In all phases of delivery including the use of my voice, I want to be as natural and authentic as possible. In addition to claiming my own sound, I try to emphasize two other matters related to the voice: pitch and pace.

The first concern is the pitch of our sound. Most of us have a range within our voice, and if we try to move outside that range, it creates problems. To avoid a monotone, I try to fluctuate within my range. Remember the power of lowering one's voice. Some of us were taught that to emphasize something in a sermon, we should raise our voices. Some people feel that true preaching requires the preacher to get red in the face and to shout. The most important things I say are usually said softly. "I love you; I care about you; I need you"—it is hard to imagine that I would yell these things.

The second matter related to the voice is the pace of the sermon. Some of the preaching students I have are preaching their first sermons, and they are nervous. I tell them that I hope they never lose some anxiety no matter how long they preach. If preachers tell me they feel no anxiety, I wonder if they realize what an awesome task we have to speak for God to the lives of people. That should make all of us tremble.

The initial nervousness new preachers feel is often seen in the rapid pace of their sermons. They are anxious to get finished and to make sure the ideas and words come in proper sequence. The result is that the phrases tumble over each other and there is little use of pause. That is why I try to get the students as well as myself to think through the sermon and to realize that there are places where we need to stop and linger and let people reflect.

The Face of Preaching: How Do I Look?

It is important to remind ourselves that people do not just listen to our words, but they listen to us. What are we communicating with our voice as well as our whole being? What does our face say? Does it reflect the grace, the joy, the judgment, or the experience of the sermon we are preaching?

Congruence is not a word often used in connection with preaching, but this concept conveys a strong significance for preaching. Preaching has congruence when all aspects of our being that convey the message are communicating the same thing. Consider for example, a message on hope. The text is Colossians 1:27 (NIV), "To them God has chosen to make known among the Gentiles the glorious riches of this mystery, which is Christ in you, the hope of glory." What a powerful word for life. The Christians of Colossae undoubtedly had times when they felt overwhelmed by the difficulties around them. Like us, they had days when the problems seemed too big and their power too meager. Then they heard this word, "Christ in you, the hope of glory." These words were likely given by Paul with all of his being showing the hope he felt in Christ for himself and all believers. That is congruence. What did those words do to the Colossians? What do those words do to us and for us?

The face of preaching is shaped as we live into the experience of a text and then attempt to convey something of that experience to our listeners. The face of our preaching should grow naturally from our encounter with the text and our own hearing of the word for our lives. In this way, we avoid two major difficulties with the face of our preaching: No emotional quality and an artificial look.

The first difficulty is when our face has no affect and reflects nothing of the emotional quality of the words we speak. Our face looks unconverted; it does not seem to have heard the things about which we speak. We preach about the ultimate things of life with a lack of passion that belies their significance. It is important to see the sermon as more than a sequence of words or a succession of phrases. If we only learn the order of the sermon, we may not feel or experience its power. The result is a flat, dispassionate delivery that talks about faith, hope, and love in the same way that we would give someone the time of day.

The other difficulty that is a part of the face of preaching is the artificial or contrived look. In the desire to look pleasant, some preachers assume a plastic smile. Again, the difficulty is that the face of this kind of preaching does not come from our experience as preachers within the text and with what we are trying to say. This face is put on, assumed, and it communicates artificiality, not authenticity.

Another aspect of the face of preaching is the use of our eyes. Eye contact is important, but this does not mean staring at our listeners. When we preach we need to move our eyes around the congregation, not just looking at one person or one section of the sanctuary.

Eyes can communicate passion and intensity. They can share reflection and questioning as well. Sometimes it is helpful to have an upward glance or to look to the side or down as if creating a space in which we shape the contours of a story. Sometimes we want the listeners to use the eyes of their heart to imagine a scene. It is, therefore, important for preachers to tell the story as if we are seeing the whole thing unfold before our eyes.

I suggest to students who use a manuscript in their preaching that they do not write out their stories or illustrations. Rather, I encourage them to concentrate on visualizing what they want to say and then give the hearers a picture of it. This moves the sermon from being just a message we hear to an experience that we hear and see.

The Hands of Preaching: How Do I Gesture?

One of the first questions I was asked by a student in a preaching class was, "Do I practice my gestures?" I remember my first experiences in preaching when I would stand in front of a mirror and practice not only what I was going to say but how I was going to say it. I would put in certain gestures and movements; I am certain at times it must have seemed like a cartoon. I even remember several sermons when I forgot to gesture at the appropriate place and later inserted the gesture into the sermon because I had liked the way it looked in the mirror.

My answer to the student's question was no. Rather, I encouraged him to think and feel his way into the sermon he was preaching and then gesture in a way that was natural to him. I suppose that "natural" is the best way to describe the gestures and movements we use. They should come out of us and out of the sermon we are preaching rather than being carefully choreographed.

When I am preaching about something with which I am struggling or sharing some personal word, I tend to use gestures that are tighter to my body and express the moving of something from inside me to those around me. If, on the other hand, I am preaching on the global mission of the church, I am more expansive in my gestures. Again, the two things that determine my gesturing are the nature of the message and what is natural for me.

After We Preach

Few things are more painful to those who preach than hearing or seeing ourselves in the act of preaching. I suppose some of that has to do with our egos. At least, I have found that true of me. My own ministerial identity was so tied up with my preaching that any criticism, whether from me or from someone else, was devastating.

I grew up wanting to be the best preacher. I am not even sure what it means to be the best preacher, but I did not want to be a good preacher or even the best preacher that I could be; I wanted to be *the best*.

Preaching may bring out the best in us at times, but it also has a way of evoking those demons of insecurity and competitiveness. I confess that I have found myself speaking at preaching conferences where I have listened to the other ministers as if they were competitors for the affection and applause of the audience, rather than viewing them as people who were sharing truths for all of our lives. The result is that preaching became a performance, and in my mind only one of us could be crowned as "best of the class."

Several years ago I started to look at what this attitude was doing to me. It was turning preaching into a self-centered experience. I was preaching to get my own need for attention met; the response I was looking for was not that people heard about Christ but that they remembered me. The sad fact is that this was not only a perversion of the intention of preaching but it was also a draining, fatiguing experience for me. Every sermon had to be better than the last, and each time I preached I was trying to be the best.

Of course, I was not the best. Even sadder was that this kept me from becoming a better preacher because criticism was not tolerated. I share this because some of the students whom I have in preaching class have difficulty accepting criticism. It is usually the ones who have some real gifts for preaching, but their egos are so involved with their preaching that they have difficulty hearing about places where they may improve.

Why not make our goal to be the best preacher that we can be? Why not set out to take the talents and gifts God has given us and develop them as much as possible? This frees us after the sermon to be open to ways that can help us be the best communicators possible.

That is why God has called us to preach. I doubt that God even has a best preacher, and if He does, it is probably not any of us who have tried to be. We preach so that people can hear the good news that God loves them in Jesus Christ. The most important words that we will ever hear from God are, "Well done, thou good and faithful servant" (Matt. 25:21, KJV). It is freeing to give the best that we can on any given Sunday and then to leave our preaching as a gift in the hands of God.

Exercises

I. Listen to or watch a tape of a sermon you have preached. Before you preached, how did you feel about the message you were going to share? Did you believe it was vitally important and needed to be heard?

II. When you were preaching, what was on your mind? Were you overly concerned about being liked or well received? Did you think that it was most important to present the message as clearly as possible and allow God to use it?

III. How did people respond to the sermon? Did anyone say anything that indicated his or her life may have been transformed? Was anything said that was negatively critical? How did you receive it? Did you take it personally? Was the criticism devastating to you, making you think you should have pursued another vocation? Did you learn from it and then forget about it?